Awaken to Rest

Daily words of comfort and hope

Sarah Kunze

Published by Chesley Press
Columbus, Georgia
Email: awaken.to.rest@gmail.com
www.AwakenToRest.net

Design and layout: Michelle Glennon, Glennon Design Group (glennondesigngroup.com)

Cover and interior art: Heni Sandoval (henisandoval.com)

Printed and bound in the United States of America
International Standard Book Number: 978-1-7377952-0-9

ESV, English Standard Version. The Holy Bible, English Standard Version Copyright © 2001 by Crossway Bibles, a publishing ministry of Good News Publishers.

NIV, New International Version. Holy Bible, New International Version ®, NIV ® Copyright © 1973, 1978, 1984, 2001 by Biblica, Inc.

NKJV, New King James Version Copyright © 1982 by Thomas Nelson.

NASB, New American Standard Bible Copyright © 1960, 1962, 1963, 1968, 1971, 1972, 1973, 1975, 1977, 1995, 2020 by the Lockman Foundation.

Author's Note

These words are transformative verse-like gems that can penetrate your heart with God's grace. His love for you is paramount and He wants us all to come into the realization of that. I have learned this by sitting morning by morning listening to the words he spoke to my hurting heart.

Gradually my self-nonacceptance started to change as His love began to sink in. My prayer is that you too will realize how greatly you are loved, that any misconception you have of yourself or God will fade away, that you will come into the knowledge you can never be separated from Him, and that His desire is for you to know of His constant concern and attention. Life is His gift to you, in Him it is a path to discover your identity as a cherished child of God.

Author's Prelude

Nothing will deter me from the beauty of the Lord and His plan and dream. I plant my flag with Lion and Lamb and declare the day has come. Now is the time. Rejoice all of heaven. Rejoice on earth. Victory is close at hand, nearer than ever before. Arise you who slumber. Awaken into His rest and see the peace and glory around you. It is you who are His glory. See your own beauty. See your own glorious life. You are the shining stone in the river of life, discovered with joy by a child for her collection. It is you who are that treasure. Open your eyes to see and your ears to hear the gentle music of heaven reverberating on earth, bringing new life and love to awaken us all.

" And I will make for them a covenant on that day with the beasts of the field, the birds of the heavens, and the creeping things of the ground. And I will abolish the bow, the sword, and war from the land, and I will make you lie down in safety. And I will betroth you to Me forever. I will betroth you to Me in righteousness and in justice, in steadfast love and in mercy. I will betroth you to Me in faithfulness. And you shall know the Lord. " Hosea 2:18-20 (ESV)

Introduction

You are in the peaceful Kingdom. It is a place
of safety and rest. Realize I guard you and
watch over you carefully. There is no reason
for fear to ever enter your life. My love is the
strongest force in the universe. It upholds you
in more ways than you know. Let these words
comfort and penetrate your heart. See them as
seeds and once planted in the garden of your
soul, I will cultivate them; the fruit of love, joy,
and peace will begin to grow and blossom.
Know you can relax in Me and trust Me. As we
spend time together, you will begin to see how
wondrous you are and realize the endless depth
of My love for you.

" For those God foreknew He also predestined to be conformed to the image of his Son, that He might be the firstborn among many brothers and sisters. "

Romans 8:29 (NIV)

January

You are on a
journey into Me.
I am here. You
can rest against
truths older than
time that you are
Mine, always
and forever.

January 1

BELIEVE THE GOOD INTENTION I HAVE FOR YOUR LIFE. You are My idea. No one else has the true authority to define you. Find your definition in Me. Allow the infinite love of My heart to correct any misconception the world has crafted within you. Focus on the Cross and let the dead things that wound you be nailed there. Come up into the resurrected life I have provided. There is victory in the new day prepared for you.

January 2

I AM THE KING OF KINGS. I preside over the universe. What seems large and impossible to you, in Me, is able to be overcome. The brokenness you have held onto can be released as you take steps with Me. The time is now. You are not a captive. I came to set you free. The Cross is where your freedom was secured. See what hurt and maimed you dying there and rise up in the resurrected life I have placed within you.

January 3

VALUE YOU. No one can take your place in Me. Perceive My divine intent to make that known to you. Your cost is immeasurable to Me. See My death on the Cross as My heart's desire for you. Resurrection was a relief to Me for I have redeemed you forever into My arms. Relax into My embrace and let all unworthiness and insecurity go for you truly are My beloved.

January 4

B E ALERT. Great things are afoot in the Kingdom. Tune into truths that are more powerful than the world's view. Your citizenship is of a different kind. Your destiny is glorious so take up shining weaponry of praise and prayer to fend off darkness. Make way for spoils of war coming to you; those you love being freed with blessing to you and yours.

January 5

ALLOW MY LOVE TO START AN AVALANCHE WITHIN YOUR HEART CAUSING ROCKS AND BOULDERS OF HURTS AND OFFENSES TO COME DOWN OPENING A NEW WAY. You will be free to explore vistas unseen before. Beautiful areas of peace and tranquility are available.

January 6

YOUR JOURNEY IS IMPORTANT. The trail of your life is in Me. Know wherever you are I am. Any misstep or mistake is redeemed in Me. Realize and gain awareness of the loving gaze of My heart upon you that never shifts. Let the warmth of My cherishment empower you onward. Learn to be a conduit of the love and acceptance that comes your way.

January 7

REST IN MY CAPABILITY FOR WE ARE JOINED TOGETHER. The immensity of who I am is at your disposal. You are more than able to take the land. No matter the giants you fear, move forward for they will give way. Declare the truth of the Cross that delivered you into new creation life. Old things are as dust and the brightness of My light is upon and within you. The darkness of the world is no match for the shining glory of a Kingdom citizen.

January 8

I HAVE PREPARED A WAY CONTRARY TO THE HECTIC SYSTEM OF WORKING HARD FOR SELF-WORTH AND APPROVAL. Living by your own strength can get you only so far. Come into My strength and find rest. A life of blessing is purposed in My heart for you. Access it by focusing on the accomplishment of the Cross. Sin and the corruption it brings, as well as the stringent code that empowered it, were rendered void. You are a new creation free under My loving influence to become the overcomer I destined you to be.

January 9

CLAIMED YOU IN MY HEART BEFORE THE FOUNDATION OF CREATION WAS LAID. I knew your day would come and rejoiced to see it. Allow the love and favor I have for you to lift you up and keep you buoyant. This river of life is yours to navigate. I have equipped you for the ride.

January 10

LIGHT IS CONTINUOUSLY SPILLING FROM MY HEART TO YOURS. Darkness does not stand a chance when you realize a resurrected existence is at your disposal. Celebrate with Me the success of the Cross. There, all that would stop the beauty of your life was done away with. Truly you are a new creation with great capacity to touch the world with your light.

January 11

URN TO ME AT ALL TIMES AND SEE THE EXPANSE OF YOUR LIFE GO FORWARD. I am the King who has called you into favor. Realize in Me the impossible is possible. You are anointed with heaven to proceed through your day. You have been selected to bear My image. Bask in My love as you are changed from glory to glory.

January 12

YOU HAVE BEEN BROUGHT FROM DEATH TO LIFE. Sun sparkling grace reigns where sin's dark cloud once ruled. Sing out songs of thanksgiving because the high-priced blood makes you clean. Never to be touched by condemnation again; liberty and love cover you. Hearken all creatures, this one has been cleansed and made anew to bring glory to the King.

January 13

D O NOT SEE ME AS FAR AWAY. I am your existence. I uphold you. My heart had a place for you before creation. You are here now because you are My choice. The isolated feeling that you are on your own is an illusion. I am nearer than your heartbeat. I hear you always. I am for you. Come into the awareness of My love that flows like a torrent for you. Be swept away into the truth that you have always been cherished.

January 14

YOU FEAR SOME MAY THINK YOU ARE DULL, BUT I FIND YOU MOST INTERESTING. You are the one I enjoy to be around. Inside you have I put wonders. As you sense My pleasure your life will glow, and others will be drawn towards you. But you must remember the ones that feel on the sideline too. Welcome them to the joy you have found.

January 15

YOU ARE VERY COSTLY TO ME. Let the Cross stand as a reminder of your value. Never demean who you are for you are joined to Me and I gladly give My approval. Sin and flaws fall away as you see yourself through My eyes. I risked all to be inseparable from you. So, rest in that union and through Me you will rule and reign in this life.

January 16

THE STRESS AND PRESSURE YOU LIVE UNDER IS NOT FROM ME. You receive this life from the world, not the Kingdom. In green fields far away, I call you to rest. Take a minute, step out of your frantic pace, and come with Me. As you visit Me here often, peace will begin to fill you. Life's weight will be lifted off your shoulders onto Mine. I love you My cherished one.

January 17

TENACIOUSLY HOLD ONTO THE VISION **I HAVE OF YOU.** Agree with Me that you have been made lovely by the blood of the Lamb. Firmly step out into your day with confidence. My grace blankets you with approval. Any thought of you that is not in love is not of Me, cast it away and receive My word that you are the beloved.

January 18

STRIVING HARD TO PLEASE ME TAKES YOUR FOCUS FROM MY ACCOMPLISHMENT IN YOU. My work declared you righteous. Your failures and sin were nailed to the Cross. I opened new life to you where the pleasure I have in you and for you can manifest. See yourself solidly secure in My heart and move through life knowing I have your back. When you fall get back up and keep going, confident that your real pristine identity in Me, I paid for, will prevail.

January 19

SEE YOURSELF THROUGH MY EYES. I envisioned you before time to be here right now. The Cross did away with all that was unlovely about you. Now you shine with My radiance that lights creation. No matter what is going on I reside deep within you and am pleased with the union I paid for. All that tries to weigh you down cannot outlast the vision I have for you. Step into the golden identity that has been planned for you eternally.

January 20

THE LOVE I HAVE FOR YOU IS INDESTRUCTIBLE. Allow it to permeate your being. You will never face your life alone for I am with you. I have made you one with Me so do not be afraid. Circumstances will come but they are all steps to Me as I orchestrate your life. Thus, go forward each day knowing deeper discovery of Me is available. Align yourself with My instruction to love and let all else fall by the wayside. Love is your origin and your destination.

January 21

I **AM FOR YOU.** Never doubt My goodness toward you. Listen for Me with open ears. Sounds of heaven are around you for you are seated in heavenly places far above the hum of the world. Set your sights on Me alone and the splendor of who I am will spill onto you. You will become a magnet attracting others to Me as you commune with Me continually.

January 22

YOU ARE MY BELOVED. I call you forth out of past defeat into new areas of growth and development. Arise from the ashes of the past. Step out onto the cool green grass into golden sunlight. Breathe in the wind of My spirit that will enliven you to new tasks which will bring Me glory. I call you this day to arise. As I called Lazareth forth I call you forth to take off the grave clothes. Be alert and ready. Enter into new territory with Me. I am at your side. Do not lose sight of that. Steady yourself and move with purpose.

January 23

SEIZE THE DAY KNOWING I PAID A HIGH PRICE FOR YOUR FREEDOM. You have been set on a rock that will not shift. Draw strength from the secure place that I am in you. Know that endless love is yours for I have eternal supply. Go forth giving out what you have received from Me.

January 24

ROYAL BLOOD, A THREAD THROUGH TIME, INTERTWINES YOU WITH ME. The Cross shines forth in victory as My blood was poured out for the world. There is life in this blood; Holy life of divine fire making you clean and pure. No stain of darkness can stay as resurrection springs forth with unstoppable power. Laughter of heaven sounds as My bloodline pulses with My love, making all who are Mine new. None can halt the good work that has begun as you are safely hidden in Me. In the cleft of the rock, you can rest and know that within you is light unimaginable.

January 25

YOU BELONG TO A KINGDOM THAT IS EVERLASTING. The world is passing but your citizenship there is forever. Keep this perspective in mind and no circumstance on earth can continuously hold you down. The eternal truth that I have placed My resurrection life within you will cause you to prevail.

January 26

LIKE THE THUNDERING HOOVES OF GALLOPING HORSES MY POWER IS WITHIN YOU. Pull upon Me for your conquest of the day. You are not weak for I have the strength of armies and have united Myself to you. Cast off all fear of defeat. Move forward toward the high call I have placed on you. My ability inside you is unlimited. Failure is powerless against the victory I am for you.

January 27

YOUR FRIENDSHIP TO ME IS VERY VALUABLE. It delights My heart when you look to Me instead of the world. What I have is more solid, real, and everlasting. Turn from any thought that does not bring life and hope. Settle in your mind that My friends are greatly cared for and rewarded.

January 28

I AM ACQUAINTED WITH YOUR SORROWS AND DISAPPOINTMENTS. I joined Myself to you at the Cross and where you go I go. Sense My presence and lean into Me for comfort. Only I intimately know your experience. Believe that I bring your deliverance. I deliver the sunrise every morning and I will break forth light into your darkness.

January 29

I **LOVE YOU.** I was torn upon the Cross so nothing could tear you from Me. Do not allow circumstances to block sight of My love. It is powerful to transform whatever is within or around you. Current fears and present obstacles will be defeated as you relentlessly focus on My heart for you.

January 30

STEP ONTO THE WATER. Know I am in you to walk a new way. Circumstances cannot drown you. You are of a new order and mountains move before you as you trust Me completely. My love is a powerful force that cannot be stopped. It is within you to finish what I have begun. Be brave; allow it to propel you into new territory where the lost will feel Me, the deaf will hear, and the blind will see by your hand.

January 31

TOGETHER WE ARE INTERTWINED FOREVER. I sought out the darkness that separated you and took it on at the Cross. I won the battle for My own. Now you are totally Mine purified before Me. So, walk in the freedom I provided. When old patterns from the past rise up stand strong in the truth that you are a new creation. Hold onto Me and they will disintegrate and lose influence. My life is the strength within you. It has the power to conform you into who I have destined you to be.

66 The Lord your God in your midst, The Mighty One, will save; He will rejoice over you with gladness, He will quiet you with His love, He will rejoice over you with singing. 99

Zephaniah 3:17 (NKJV)

February

This time with you is
precious to Me. My
life is yours to enjoy.
Feel the warmth of My
presence as you peer
into truths that can
liberate you from any
misconception of Me.

February 1

YOUR LIGHT IS BEAUTIFUL TO ME.
Do not let the mixed messages of the world determine your value. Open your heart to receive the love that called you into existence. I preplanned you before creation and rejoice that you are here now. As you tune into My delight of you, having to constantly prove your worth is unnecessary. Rest in My acceptance and a good life will unfold.

February 2

THE POWER FOR GOOD HAS BEEN GIVEN TO YOU AS MY CHOSEN. Carefully consider the impact you create with your life. Be a catalyst of light wherever you go. The spark in you can ignite love and hope in others. Know the Kingdom is advanced in the thoughtful and kind steps you take.

February 3

*Y*OU ARE HERE NOW, RIGHT AT THIS TIME, TO BE A BEAUTIFUL EXPRESSION OF WHO I CREATED YOU WITHIN MYSELF TO BE. You are not on your own. There is no separation that leaves you hanging. Love undergirds every point of your existence. Be brave to show forth your true identity for you are created to be a valid and necessary part.

February 4

TAKE THOUGHT OF THE ENORMITY OF YOUR IMPORTANCE TO ME. I embraced the Cross to be able to embrace you. Any inferior feelings must give way. Your value is not established by your performance but by My love. When you have failings, it does not mar your worth. I am in you and capable to beautify your life. Rest in Me and allow My work to come forth.

February 5

PLACE YOUR CONFIDENCE IN ME. I am reliable. The news of the day changes but I do not. I am the foundation you need in turbulent times. The secure residence of My heart is safe, and you are welcome there always.

February 6

O NOT BE DISTRACTED BY THE NEGATIVE, FOCUS ON THE BLESSING OF WHO I AM IN YOUR LIFE. As you do, light will come and dispel the darkness of your situation. To rule and reign you must stand in the victory I won for you at the Cross. See yourself within My resurrection and ascension above the circumstances that try to pin you down in discouragement. Breathe in the encouragement of heaven and move forward believing the best and the best will open up before you.

February 7

I PLACED ETERNITY IN YOUR HEART TO DRAW YOU TO ME. I am what you need. Look away from the sin and the woes of the world to the new creation I have formed you to be. Shine with heaven's light, for your true place is there. Walk in what I have provided by My sacrifice. You have been freed to shine in the glorious splendor of who I am in you. All creation is waiting.

February 8

MY LOVE IS TRANSFORMATIONAL.
You are not who you were. Now you
are full of My life, resurrection life, to bring renewal
to those around you. So, set yourself ablaze with
the love I have for you. Burn brightly bringing light
to those in darkness and providing warmth for the
cold ones who are outside the knowledge of Me.
You are My beautiful flame. The colors of who I am
flash within you.

February 9

L ET ME BATHE THE PLACE IN YOUR HEART THAT HURTS WITH MY LIGHT. Come to Me when you are wounded. Allow Me to settle your soul. Wrap yourself in My kindness. The healing balm of My presence is here for you always.

February 10

YOU ARE CALLED TO A WAY OF LIFE THAT REFLECTS THE BEAUTY OF WHO I AM. The righteousness gifted to you empowers you to do that. Cleansed by My blood, and indwelled by My love, move forward daily extending the kindness I have shown to you. My crucifixion dealt a death blow against any force that would keep you from achieving this. You are more than able to be the light I destined you to be.

February 11

ANY ALIENATION YOU FEEL IS NOT FROM ME. The world can be cold and cruel. You must become aware of the fire of My love within you that cannot be extinguished. I welcomed you in My heart before creation. I care about the intricacies of your life. Become aware that your real home is the Kingdom, a place of acceptance and light. Sense your value as a citizen there. The part you play is important. I validated you with the cost of My life.

February 12

BE VALIANT! My love has persevered through death for you. You can stand with thankfulness and declare that you are free. Temporary circumstances of darkness cannot overcome you for you were singled out in My heart before the foundation of the world. My Kingdom is your true home and the world's negative influence will have no lasting impact.

February 13

AS RUSHING WATER OF A RIVER AFTER A STORM, MY SPIRIT IS WITHIN YOU FLOWING POWERFULLY. It will take away old debris that blocked you from the knowledge of Me. Bravely dive into the water of My affection. There is freedom from the shore of stagnation to gloriously ride the adventure of My love.

February 14

B E WHO YOU ARE. I have faith in the beauty I originated before the foundation of the earth for you to be. Do not give in to dark imaginations that cloud the vision I see of you. The Cross reveals that your nearness to Me is something I valued with My life to have. Freely enjoy who you are because I am with you.

February 15

BEFORE THE STARS WERE FRAMED IN THE SKY YOU WERE A LIGHT IN MY HEART. I destined you to shine. So regardless of how you feel there is a brightness that only you can add to your surroundings. Your part is substantial. Your importance to Me is more than you can fathom.

February 16

LLOW MY KINDNESS TO UNDO WHAT WAS DONE TO HARM YOU. All along I have been with you. The Cross shows My unity with you in the midst of your pain. Hold on with hope. There is a sunrise coming. Darkness cannot outlast My love. Resurrection life is My gift to you. It will recreate and beautify your life.

February 17

THE LIQUIDNESS OF MY LOVE; LET IT FILL YOU DAILY. My heart is alive with your expression. Your movement into My love delights Me. Keep coming for a drink of who I am in you. As you do you will flourish into a tree of strength and beauty where others can find shade and rest from the heat of their afflictions.

February 18

THE SUNSET CLOSES OUT THE DAY. Leave behind the mistakes and missteps therein. Opportunities for fresh beginnings are built into the existence I provide. Listen to the birdsong in the morning and let optimism fill your heart. New choices are before you in the day to come.

February 19

O NOT DRAW YOUR IDENTITY FROM YOUR PLACE IN THE WORLD BUT FROM THE PLACE YOU HAVE IN MY HEART. My love strengthens and clarifies your life. Depending on the world's acclaim will weaken and confuse you. Fixation on the idols of this age will tarnish your beauty. You are made in My image. Focus on Me to see the wonder of who you truly are.

February 20

THE QUALITY OF YOUR LIFE MATTERS TO ME. Filter out old critical dark thoughts through the lens of My love. Begin to believe the best and always hope for the good. I promise transformation will come as you do. My creative force is within you to bring forth a beautiful reality.

February 21

OUR PRAISE AND THANKSGIVING CREATE A PLATFORM FOR YOU TO WALK FORTH INTO YOUR DAY ABOVE CIRCUMSTANCES THAT WOULD DERAIL YOU. As your focus, I lead you into places you would not get to on your own. Keep your words continually honoring Me and My provision will open up to you in ways that will bring great joy.

February 22

FORGET ABOUT OFFENSES. They block the life that is meant to flow and grow within you. The staleness of a grudge is like a room that needs an open window. Pull back the shades, lift the window up, and let the breeze come in. The freshness takes away the dank dark drabness. The gentle wind and light begin to fill your dwelling. You can see clearly and breathe clean air again.

February 23

FOREVER YOUR LIFE IS SECURED BY ME. I intend to see you through the circumstances you encounter. You are hidden safely in My heart. Glide through your day with ease knowing that you are looked after carefully. When difficulty arises be still and sink into the cushion of My love. Remember the truth, that all things work together for good for those whose hearts are Mine.

February 24

REST IN WHAT WAS DONE FOR YOU AT THE CROSS. The love I showed for you there cannot be stopped. Allow it to infiltrate your perception of how valuable you are. You are a jewel in My heart. See yourself as such. Reflect the beauty of who you are into the world. Decorate the life of those around you with love.

February 25

YOU HAVE HELD ONTO THE PLACE IN YOURSELF WHERE YOU FEEL UNLOVELY. I say it is time to let go and reach out to hold onto only Me. My victory on the Cross was given to you. Step in and receive it. Failure and lack must go. Ascended life is My gift to you. Rise up and walk in it.

February 26

SEE YOURSELF IN ME UPON THE CROSS AND THE SINS THAT BESET YOU WILL BE RENDERED POWERLESS. The sinner identity is no longer who you are. Righteousness, empowered by grace, enlightens you. A life of goodness flows from you naturally. I embrace you fully as My own; My special ornament to beautify the world.

February 27

NOURISH YOURSELF WITH THE GOOD THOUGHTS I HAVE FOR YOU. I say you are worthy and are a unique treasure to Me. Your quality comes from Me for I am your Maker. My design is flawless. My purpose for you was known before time. Your importance to Me is reflected in the price of My blood. Never belittle who I call priceless.

February 28

YOUR POINT OF VIEW IS NOT MORE IMPORTANT THAN ANOTHER PERSON'S. Smugness and superiority do not belong in the Kingdom. Caring and kindness supersede any proofs and theories that separate and demean. Hear the love cry of the Cross that echoes through time and know the worth of each individual. Realize your disdain for others is not acceptable.

February 29

O NOT FEEL BORING OR UNAPPEALING. My intricate plan to enter into human life and take on sin and defeat it was for you. You were worth the Cross. Shift your focus from why you do not qualify to the fact that I qualified you to shine in a way that only you can do for you. You are chosen and placed into My royal race. Learn that you can rule and reign in the light of My love. Your destiny has the power of the King behind it.

66 You will show me the path of life; in Your presence is fullness of joy; at Your right hand are pleasures forevermore. 99

Psalm 16:11 (NKJV)

March

I want you to remember
you are not alone on the
path you travel. Within
you, I wait for your
realization of Me and
My love that empowers
your life.

March 1

W HEN DARKNESS DESCENDS, REALIZE
I AM HERE, AND THE LIGHT OF
MY LOVE NEVER GOES OUT. Trials are part of
existence, but I am with you as you journey. The
green grass blade comes up after the dead of winter.
New life, hidden now, will arise. Trust Me to see
you through to a bright horizon.

March 2

XTEND THE CIRCLES OF LOVE IN YOUR LIFE. I have included all, and your inclusion of others delights My heart. The damaging behavior of exclusion and rejection is not the way of the Kingdom. All are welcome. There is great joy when a lonely soul is touched by your love.

March 3

YOUR IMPORTANCE TO ME IS NOT DEBATABLE. The Cross indicates your value. My choice and action speak volumes and no other philosophy affirms you the way I do. Worldly wisdom and religion, devoid of the reality of the Cross, are empty promises. My promise of redemption and restoration through death and resurrection is the sustaining principle of the universe. I am the genuine source who gives quality and truth to your life.

March 4

THE HORSE WITH STRENGTH AND BEAUTY GALLOPS UNDER THE MOONLIGHT. The sounds of hooves alert you that I am coming. No longer will you be locked in your torment, for I will break down the door, untie you, and bring you into freedom.

March 5

BASK IN THE SUNLIGHT OF MY PRESENCE. As you do, My words that are strong and mighty will arise in your heart. They will do battle against hurtful and destroying shadows that try to cast their gloom of death upon you. Into the light, flowers of grace and beauty will come forth as you lean only into Me. Colorful arrays will dot the landscape with My love. Blooms will send forth beautiful fragrances. Stay in the goodness of who I am and the darkness will have no influence over you.

March 6

KINDNESS IS WHAT I VALUE; INCORPORATE IT INTO YOUR BEING. Let it bathe you from the throne room where I pour it forth daily. Then walk it out with others in your midst that need relief from any cruelty that has touched their life.

March 7

BE FUELED BY ME. Drop the self-striving. Apart from Me you make nothing lasting. You will reign in life when you cease from your own works. Enter into My accomplishment at the Cross, from where you arose with Me into resurrection life. See My sufficiency within you. Learn to rest in the security of who I am in you.

March 8

CEASE FROM THE DOWNWARD TRAIL OF NEGATIVE THOUGHTS. Instead, focus on the path above where the light of the Kingdom shines. Declarations of My accomplishment for you will transform the dark place you have settled for. The Cross truly delivered you. Resurrection life is yours as you embrace your union in Me.

March 9

DO NOT BE A PART OF EXCLUSION.
I came to be a friend and call you to the same standard. There is no one "less than" in My Kingdom. The rankings of the world do not dictate or apply to you for in My eyes all have tremendous value. Extend My favor and acceptance to everyone you meet and the light I am in you will shine brightly.

March 10

~

YOU ARE IN MY HEART SAFELY SECURED BY MY LOVE. It is a real place; more real than the alone and isolating feelings you experience. Take My nail scarred hand and enter through the Cross into the reality of our union.

March 11

COMPETITION IS NOT THE WAY OF THE CROSS. You have been joined with Me. Rest in My acceptance and cease from striving to be significant. You gladly cost Me My life. My blood washed away the need for you to prove your worth to others. Instead, soak up My love and flow in the liberating light of the security that is yours in Me.

March 12

∽

YOU ARE MY EXPRESSION FOREVER.
I have invested all I am into you. See
Me within as a source of living water, washing any
lie of separation away. Quench your thirst with the
sparkling liquid light of My love. True satisfaction is
yours as you do.

March 13

YOU ARE A MESSAGE OF LIGHT IN MY GARDEN. I selected and appointed you for this time. The magnificence of the moment is that we are joined in union. Your awareness of that can impact others. The lie of isolation will dissolve in them as they encounter the Tree of Life in you.

March 14

LOVE OVERRIDES YOUR NEED TO BE RIGHT. A person is more important than an idea or a theory. Arrogance does not reflect the Cross. Within Me, find the humility that can truly bring change to those around you. A gentle and humble spirit is stronger than a prideful one. Cease from your superiority and walk the way of the Kingdom.

March 15

I WANT YOU TO KNOW YOUR VALUE. The beauty of the sunset is for you. The birdsong in the morning sings out My love for you each day. The wagging of the dog's tail and the cat's purr is to warm your heart. The tree's brilliant colors in autumn and the fragrance of springtime blossoms were designed with you in mind. My image and likeness are upon you, My chosen one. Your significance is as large as the universe I created for you.

March 16

I **AM LOYAL AND TRUE.** You may forget Me for long lengths of time, but you are not forgotten by Me. My eye attends to you always. I am patient and await your call. Then I will open your eyes to see I am always here with the answers you need.

March 17

I EXPERIENCED SHAME SO YOU WOULD NOT BE ALONE IN YOURS. But when you came into the Kingdom shame lost its address. So do not hold onto it, but place it carefully where it belongs, on the Cross. You have entered into a resurrected purified life. My waterfall of favor flows over you continually. You are eternally accepted. So, lift your head up and realize the significance you have in My heart.

March 18

TEND TO YOUR HEART; ONLY LET PRAISE AND THANKSGIVING COME FROM YOUR LIPS. The negative things will lose fuel as you accentuate your blessings. I am good regardless of circumstances. Hold and nourish that thought through all that you encounter, and you will triumph. I am the triumphant one and your position is in Me.

March 19

B E AWARE OF THE HURTING HEARTS AROUND YOU. Any exclusion that wounds is not the way of the Kingdom. Kindness and inclusion to the different one is My hopeful expectation. The warmth of My love for you is to aid in bringing others in, out of the cold.

March 20

TAKE THE TIME TO SHARE IN THE CHAIN OF LIGHT I DEMONSTRATED. Your kindness and consideration leave great beauty in their wake. Darkness in the hearts of others will recede into the colors of a sunrise. I paint the sky for you, a great promise every day. Know your life can color with loveliness the lives of those around you.

March 21

YOU ARE THE LIGHT IN MY EYE. I saw you before time. Everything that hurt and defamed you was placed on Me on the Cross. I bore it into the grave, rising with you, cleansed, and made ready for eternity. Always connect your heart with Mine and pull on My powerful love that can shape you into the beautiful light giver I have planned you to be.

March 22

DO NOT FEEL ALONE IN THIS WORLD. The ache you have in your heart connects you to the Cross where I identified with you. I encapsulated all the pain of isolation and separation and took it to the grave. From there I arose in union with you. Nothing can take you from Me. My love is a strong cord that holds us together.

March 23

NO MATTER WHAT YOU GO THROUGH, I AM HERE. I have what you need. Let Me impart My light into the darkness that would try to overcome you. Rise up with the resurrection life within you. I overcame death so you could come to new heights. Leave the tormenter behind as you acknowledge the union we share. You are safe under the shadow of My wing. Breathe in the power of redemption. You are righteous and shine with My glory. All accusers must be silenced. Listen only to Me; I say you are My beloved and I am pleased.

March 24

O COME INTO YOUR REALM AND LIVE AMONG YOU WAS MY DESIRE. To link destiny with you was My intent all along. You were the treasure I sought and bought with My own blood. You matter, so discard any belief system that makes you feel insignificant. My action reveals your importance.

March 25

KNOW THAT I AM ON YOUR SIDE. Persevere into who I am calling you to be. I had you in My heart before creation. Receive My love for you into the depths of who you are. Allow it to take root and grow. It will overcome any lie that would tarnish the truth that you are made in My image to radiate Me.

March 26

YOU ARE MY ENJOYMENT. The Cross took away all separation. Feel My delight that I have made you anew. Forget your weaknesses and faults. Instead, have tunnel vision for Me alone. Trust that shortcomings cannot halt My immense power to transform you. Laugh and rejoice in the good plan I have for you.

March 27

I TEND TO MY OWN AND I HAVE BOUGHT YOU AT A GREAT PRICE. Your life is not to be lived alone, as I joined Myself to you with a powerful love. Do not venture out unaware of My presence. See Me in all that you do. Know that My plan is at work to perfect you. You can cease from all self-striving and stress as you abide in Me.

March 28

NEVER FEEL CONDEMNED, FOR RIGHTEOUSNESS SHINES FORTH FROM YOU. It is a permanent gift. I accomplished the letter of the law on your behalf. When you fail, declare My love for you and remember the Cross silenced the accuser. Go forward always expecting goodness to follow you for you have been chosen by Me. A royal bloodline now includes you. So, walk in the awareness of your heavenly lineage and you will reign with grace and beauty in this life.

March 29

WHEN YOU SEE SOMETHING UGLY IN YOURSELF REALIZE IT HAS BEEN NAILED TO THE CROSS AND YOU CAN WALK FREE. I am greater in you than the leftover lineage of Adam. You have been translated into My bloodline. So, stand with confidence. Our union is stronger than anything that comes against you. Persevere for you are a new creation and I have equipped you with My own righteousness. I am the highest royalty and I say you are My beloved. Do not think anything less.

March 30

I EMBRACED THE PAIN OF THE CROSS BECAUSE I SAW YOU AND HEARD YOUR CRY. To be your deliverer was My greatest desire. The torment that you are experiencing will pass. In the meantime, know I am with you and share in the depth of where you are. Rest in Me and in My confidence that resurrection is coming. Truly, the light of a new day is at hand.

March 31

SETTLE DOWN, MY LOVE. Do not let your heart race. I am right here with you. Turn to Me and allow Me to bring comfort to you. The world would have you running in circles with whispers of inadequacy. Close off that voice and hear Me when I say you are more than adequate. You are moving with Me to great things. Take hold of My hand and walk steadily with Me. I am here. See Me in the inner place where you truly dwell, safely in the presence of My throne. Allow My peaceful rule to guide you in all you do.

" Your love, Lord, reaches to the heavens, Your faithfulness to the skies. Your righteousness is like the highest mountains, Your justice like the great deep. You, Lord, preserve both people and animals. How priceless is your unfailing love, O God! People take refuge in the shadow of Your wings. "

Psalm 36:5-7 (NIV)

April

Listen within your heart
to the ancient call of love
that will draw you to Me.
Within Me are depths of
comfort and safety that
will enfold you forever.

April 1

SONGBIRDS RELEASE MUSIC IN THE MORNING AS A NEW DAY ARRIVES. Arise with a knowing that My joy is upon you. Face circumstances feeling My pleasure. Hum continuous praises in your heart for whatever comes. I am weaving all musical chords into a majestic chorus.

April 2

I TOOK YOU WITHIN MY HEART ON MY JOURNEY FROM DEATH TO LIFE TO TRANSFORM YOU. Newly made you can thrive. Never feeling good enough is no longer your mode. My accomplishment on the Cross has put you on a different plane. Freedom pours into your life like light through a window when you realize there is no condemnation from the One who sustains you and paid for your liberty.

April 3

OU CAN PREVAIL FOR I LIVE INSIDE OF YOU. Rise up from fear and doubt for you have risen with Me in the victory I had over the grave. Look down on circumstances that do not line up with this heavenly perspective and command them to align with My Kingdom. I safeguard you and establish you in the truth you decree by faith.

April 4

BE ALERT TO HEAR ONLY ME FOR WHAT I SAY IS WHAT MATTERS. Dark lies will come. Do not allow them to light. Firmly send them away. Golden truths shine with beauty and will enliven you. Set your mind on them alone and stay the course through your day. Forever near to you I am only a glance away. Do not stare or ponder dark things when the Light giver is at your side. Lean on Me and I will steady you. Draw your power completely from Me for I have unlimited supply.

April 5

I GAVE MY LIFE AT THE CROSS FOR YOUR
FREEDOM. A new way opened up. Sin's
control was broken and the law with the relentless
dos and don'ts was nailed there. You are not at the
mercy of shoulds and ought-tos. Instead allow
your behavior to flow from the love I have for
you. Harness My kindness and it will propel your
life. Legalistic self-striving and self-promotion will
subside into a grace filled self-giving existence.

April 6

YOUR KINDNESS IS LIKE GOLD; IT ENRICHES THE LIVES OF THOSE AROUND YOU. Be aware of the poverty of the hearts nearby. Give thoughts to those beyond yourself and true wealth will come into your life. Know My good intentions for humanity are made alive in your actions.

April 7

I AM YOUR HELP AND WITHIN REACH AT ALL TIMES. You have been sealed with love that is impenetrable. No one can tear you from Me, for I have selected you and I fiercely protect My own. You are preserved in Me forever. No matter the circumstances you face, your good is My plan. Rest in the fact that you are Mine and My love has no bounds.

April 8

O NOT LET YOUR FEELINGS RUN DOWN DARK CORRIDORS OF ANXIETY AND FEAR. Catch them and release them in the open window I always provide. Turn on the light as you enter into the expansive room of My love, a beautiful space of majesty and wonder where I reside with you. Be invigorated as you rest in the luxury and warmth of My presence. When you venture out, know that I go with you and together we can face any obstacle.

April 9

I AM IN YOU AND YOU ARE IN ME. The depth of that connection goes on eternally. Nothing is closer to you in the earth realm. United with a divine bloodline you are of a heavenly order. Walk out in faith that water will turn to wine and bread will multiply in your daily circumstances. You are called to flourish as you are gloriously entwined with the King of Kings.

April 10

RELINQUISH ALL FEAR AND LEAN INTO ME FOR I CAN ESCORT YOU FROM THE DREAD OF THE MOMENT. My love is very powerful and can transform your situation into a steppingstone to greater, more joyful times to come. Remember the shell of sin is cracked and fell from you as you received Me. You are righteous and it is My desire to bless you.

April 11

LEAVE THE SHAME YOU HAVE FELT AT THE CROSS. Come with Me through to resurrection. Realize your life shines with the light of a new day. Discard the fig leaves that hide the beauty of who I see you to be. Any poor definition of who you are is a lie. The truth is you are My chosen; one of royalty with incalculable worth.

April 12

I HAVE CHOSEN YOU TO BE PUT IN MY GARDEN. As a flower leans into the sunlight, lean into Me for I love you. Let My warmth fill your heart so you can bloom and blossom. Your fragrance will be sweet and your colors brilliant and you will bring joy to passersby.

April 13

YOU SHINE IN MY HEART. The pursuit of you was determined before the foundation of creation was laid. My rescue of you at the Cross is a testimony of your value. Life without you was not an option for Me.

April 14

WHEN YOU FEEL YOU HAVE TO MEASURE UP, COME TO ME. Allow Me to ease the perpetual disappointment you have with yourself. You caught My eye before creation. The delight of you is real in My heart. Drop out of the race to be approved and sense My approval. I translated you from darkness into My Kingdom of Light. Rejection is not in my vocabulary. The rule here is acceptance and love. Learn to rest in the immense value I place on you.

April 15

THE BIRDSONG IS THE GREETING OF A NEW DAY. Hear the constancy in the sound I ordained from the beginning. Creation surrounds you to lead you to Me. Look into the corners and crevices and you will see My imprint. Look to the stars and see the reflection of My glory. Let your song be heard. Sound the message that to deny Me is to deny the quality of your own existence.

April 16

Y RIGHTEOUSNESS IS YOURS. Nothing can penetrate it. Your life is valued and protected; sealed by My Holy blood. Know that grace outruns any sin that would want to claim you. You have been freed forever from death's domain.

April 17

FOR SUCH A TIME AS THIS, YOU HAVE BEEN BORN INTO THE KINGDOM. Your arrival here was predestined. You are well received, and your position is secure. So, embrace your days with courage knowing the good choices you make will reverberate with golden impact to the world around you.

April 18

NFATHOMABLE LOVE IS COMING TO YOU AS YOU EMBRACE THE DAY BEFORE YOU. Never before has there been someone who is you. Planned in My heart before creation you are selected to walk out this gift of life. Paid for with precious blood, you are now a part of an incorruptible bloodline. You have been called into royalty. Know you are destined to reign.

April 19

I CAN SORT OUT WHAT IS BEFORE YOU. The impossibilities are not as real as they seem. Commit your way to Me and take a step. Leave behind the doubts and move steadily with Me. My power created the universe, and I am within you and at your side. Rest in our relationship and everything else will come into place.

April 20

THE WORLD WILL SCAR HOW YOU SEE YOURSELF. So, intend in your heart to carry the image I have of you. I highly esteem you for I went to the Cross for you. My accomplishment there accomplished great things for you. Your old life was exchanged for a glorious new one. You have become royal. You are included at the highest level, always welcomed in the throne room.

April 21

TAKE HOLD OF A QUALITY THAT BELONGS TO ME. My righteousness is yours. I have given it to you. As an impenetrable robe wear it with the realization that in the depths and the heights sin can no longer clothe you.

April 22

YOU WILL NOT FIND YOUR IDENTITY IN CHASING IMAGES OF THE WORLD. They are constantly changing while I am the same yesterday, today, and always. Draw your source from Me. The Cross shows the high price of your worth so any insignificant thought you have of yourself is deceptive. You do not have to strive to be self-important. Instead rest in the importance you have in My heart. As you do, true quality will come forth into your life.

April 23

I AM HERE FOR YOU IN THE DARKNESS. Remember on the Cross My physical heart stopped beating for you. When I resurrected you were safely within My breast and carried up with My ascension. From on high you are together with Me. Allow that vantage point to be your view and your circumstances will come into the right perspective. Have faith that the light of heaven will shine into your situation.

April 24

I AM JOINED TO YOU. When fear comes, tell it that the Creator of the expanse of the heavens lives inside your heart and there is no room for it to stay. Fear shouts lies but I have the truth. My support of you is eternal and outlasts anything fear brings. It will be stopped and turned away as your reliance on Me grows stronger and stronger.

April 25

SIN IS NOT YOUR FRIEND. In fact, I went to the Cross because it was your mortal enemy. It was emptied there of its power to separate you from Me. But do not invite it to be a part of your life. Realize its design is to harm you. I am in you now. Focus on that and sin will be repelled and flee into the darkness, as My light enlightens your way.

April 26

I **AM HERE FOR YOU IN A WAY THAT NO OTHER CAN BE.** I conceived you in My heart long ago. You are an expression of My dream. Therefore, harness the joy I have over you to propel you to victory. Never doubt the high quality I see in your life and the wonderful possibilities that await you.

April 27

COME TO ME AND I WILL SORT OUT THE CONCERNS THAT DOG YOU. My peace extends into eternity and is here for you at all times. Quit allowing voices of discouragement to paint your outlook. I can undo any tangle that you have gotten into. Listen to Me. Do what I say, and you will find solutions.

April 28

YOU WERE MADE TO BLOSSOM. Do not be discouraged in the barren times. Know the vision I had in My heart for you, before creation, is within your reach. Your destiny was joined with Me on resurrection day. You arose with Me to great possibilities. The garden of life needs your color and your design. You are able to come forth.

April 29

YOU CAN CHANGE AS YOU REALIZE THE GREAT PLACE YOU HAVE IN MY HEART. The hurts you have caused and the mistakes you made are not greater than I am. I am fair to all. I soothe, restore, and rejuvenate. My resurrection life within you is powerful, enabling you to move forward in new ways. Realization of your union with Me creates vibrancy; old patterns crumble and an overcoming life of beauty and kindness will arise.

April 30

I AM HERE, I ALWAYS HAVE BEEN, AND I ALWAYS WILL BE. Sink into this truth and rest. The light in you can never be extinguished. You are with Me safe in My heart forever. Smile for the brightness in you eliminates the darkness.

" But let all those rejoice who put their trust in You; let them ever shout for joy, because You defend them; let those also who love Your name be joyful in You. For You, O Lord, will bless the righteous; with favor You will surround him as with a shield. "

Psalm 5:11-12 (NKJV)

May

Resting against each other
My heart is touched in a
way you cannot imagine.
My delight is you. Your
protection is My job. When
you see that, true freedom
in the world you live in will
arise.

May 1

TRUST MY LOVE FOR YOU REGARDLESS OF THE SITUATION. Set your face towards Me even in the darkness. My redemption of you is there every moment. And My rescue of you at the Cross is more powerful than any circumstance. The stone is moved away from the tomb and resurrection life is in you to lead you to victory. You will prevail.

May 2

N ME THERE IS NO DARKNESS. Come to Me to find the light in your situation. I am here. My vantage point will lift you from the narrow confines of your fearful perception. The expanse within Me is yours to move out in freedom. Take steps aware of My love and you will find life opening up in marvelous dimensions.

May 3

IT IS NEVER TOO LATE. You have never gone too far. Know I am here within you. My strength upholds the universe and I say you are Mine. Learn to rest from your frantic heart that has been propelled by darkness. The Cross is here; I bore your shame. Come up into the innocence I paid for. Relinquish any twisted thought and tap only into My love. It will bubble into a flow that will wash away any debris of your life and replenish the dry places.

May 4

BUTTERFLY WINGS SPLASH COLOR INTO THE AIR AS NEW CREATION REALITIES ARE YOURS. Born into the Kingdom where your life has ascended with Me your residence is above. In lightness of heart rejoice in your day.

May 5

YOU ARE VALIDATED BY MY LOVE. Your self-effort to be acknowledged must give way to the self-awareness of My life in you. Lean not on your own strivings but learn to rest in Me. You are a seed in My garden. I will cause you to rise from the ground into a flower of beauty with life giving fragrance.

May 6

SURRENDER EVERYTHING THAT DENIES THE TRUTH THAT YOU ARE LOVED. Take a stand in My heart that beats for you. Like a roaring lion I will devour the lies that taunt you. Nothing in all of creation can separate you from My intense love. Breathlessly realize that you are My desire, and you were born to thrive in My sight.

May 7

STOP ACTIONS THAT DO NOT BRING LIFE. I call you to a higher standard than self-gratification. My life was laid down for you so you could enter a life of quality. Your dissatisfaction stems from a constant focus on you and your own desires. Realize that the fulfillment you seek comes when your life extends beyond the narrow confines of self. See the Cross as My heart for all humanity. Enlarge your vision to the needs of others. Give of yourself and you will find a wonderful new way.

May 8

FEAR IS NOT YOUR FRIEND. I am. Fear offers nothing but My offering brought you from darkness into light. Shadows flee as you realize the brightness of who I am in you. The small space where fear held you captive will give way to the sunlit open expanse of My love within which solutions arise.

May 9

YOU HAVE NEVER BEEN HIDDEN FROM ME. I see you and the sterling quality of who you are. The world can cruelly and impersonally travel by. But I am with you on every step, united to you by My own desire. You are the focus of My love no matter how rejected or unacceptable you feel at times. Tune into My attention and love. It will enlighten you to the truth that you are destined to bring transformation to the same world that cruelly passes others by.

May 10

AM AT WORK IN THE OTHERS IN YOUR
LIFE. Align with Me and see the best.
Do not judge them harshly as I went to the Cross
for each one. Their value is of great worth. To mar
My character within you by your criticism is not the
way of the Kingdom. Love there is gentle and long
suffering.

May 11

I AM IN EVERY MOMENT WITH YOU.
When you are cut to the quick by the pain in life, know we are joined. The death I experienced on the Cross knew no bounds and included your hurt. I received it into Myself and resurrected to new life with you. You are safely within Me. I encompass you with love. Allow it to comfort you through the darkness until the dawn of the truth of My resurrection comes forth within you.

May 12

YOUR KINDNESS TO OTHERS MEANS A GREAT DEAL TO ME. I delight in words and actions that bring life. Carefully navigate around those broken within your reach with the Cross in mind. My blood spilt expresses how much they are cherished. The love I give to you is meant to be poured out upon them.

May 13

YOUR ATTEMPTS TO BE SELF-IMPORTANT ARE UNNECESSARY. The fact that I am your source validates who you are. Abide in the truth that I qualify you. You are meant to thrive in the identity I held in My heart for you before creation. You are a unique treasure and by resting in Me and My love you cannot help but shine.

May 14

I AM IN YOU, NOT FAR AT ALL. I paid a great price to be here. Death was no match for My love. The Cross was My journey to you. There the barrier of sin came down. You are not alone, and sin is powerless against the redemption I paid for. Keep your focus on Me and the union we share, and you will rise up in every area of your life.

May 15

THE SLURS OF A BROTHER CAN CUT DEEP.
Your life is precious to Me, so much so that
I walked where you have and deeper into the pain of
sin and rejection. The Cross is My statement to you
that I understand. Look to Me to find the healing
ointment you need. My blood continuously washes,
cleanses, and heals life's wounds. Enter into My
forgiveness as well; allow it to be a force in you to set
you free from any trap laid. Liberation is yours as
you ascend to My vantage point. All is well as you
settle into My heart that beats for you.

May 16

I AM THE SOURCE YOU NEED TO PULL FROM. You originated in Me. I have answers and am with you as you deliberate the problems that come your way. You are never alone. As surely as the sun comes up over the horizon your situation will become clear. It will be ironed out as you choose to rest in the reality of My overriding love and wisdom.

May 17

WHEN YOU SENSE DISAPPOINTMENT, IT IS NOT MINE. I always believe the best. My care for you extends beyond your behavior. Mistakes do not determine your life. Align your heart with Mine that loves you regardless. Believe in the opportunity for you to change with the new morning I provide each day. Your past is not the master of your future. Lean into Me and the course of your life will straighten out.

May 18

REST IN MY GOODNESS NO MATTER THE MISTAKES YOU HAVE MADE. On the Cross we were united eternally. The force of My love can undo the effects of the missteps you have taken. Learn to trust Me. My resurrection life within you brings transformation. I am the God of new beginnings and fresh starts. Look forward with a heart of hope and you will not be disappointed.

May 19

THE CROSS STANDS AS A TESTIMONY. Death's dark chains could not keep you from the strength of My love. The grave's cold silence gave way to resurrection song. Gathered within Me, you arose free from the mortal enemy of sin. Know that that victory is yours every day. We are joined; you contain My light and cannot be bonded to darkness again.

May 20

ABOLISH FEAR IN YOUR HEART BY REALIZING MY LOVE IS STRONGER. Fear cannot withstand eternal truths. Acknowledge you have a Kingdom destiny, and all things are working together for your good. Then place your foot upon the neck of fear and continually declare My victory. Resurrection power will rise within you with courage in its wake.

May 21

WHEN FEARFUL THOUGHTS AND NEGATIVITY COME, REMEMBER MY RESURRECTION LIFE IS WITHIN YOU. I, who defeated the grave, have given you what you need to combat these forces. They are powerless against Me and you are in Me. We are united as one. They were nailed to the Cross and left behind as you rose with Me to new life. Set your face towards Me and look not to the right or to the left. As you do you will be transformed into My likeness.

May 22

LIKE THE PREPARATION FOR A BANQUET, I HAVE PREPARED GREAT THINGS FOR YOU. You must not feel that I am disappointed in you. It is the opposite. Open the door. See the colorful banners, the silver goblets, and the crystal plates. This is your occasion. I find you worthy. Never again feel you are not welcomed.

May 23

I AM ON THE JOURNEY WITH YOU. You are not alone. Each step you take toward life I applaud. Favor, shield like, surrounds you. You are safe in the redemption I paid for. Move forward knowing anything destructive from your past has been cut off. As a new creation you are free to explore beautiful possibilities. Lies of failure and lack no longer apply. The wealth of who you are in Me will manifest as you rest in the richness of who I am in you.

May 24

*Y*OU HAVE A PURPOSE THAT FLOWS FROM THE THRONE ROOM OF My LOVE. Walk out your destiny in close contact with Me. I am the one source you need. My glory will shine upon you as you fix your eyes on Me. You are meant to radiate My life. As you plummet the depth of My love, the rich treasures you find will bring wealth to all around you.

May 25

THE WORLD'S INROAD TO YOUR LIFE THAT WOUNDS YOU CAN BE HALTED AND REVERSED BY THE POWERFUL LOVE I HAVE. Allow the balm of My presence to soothe and heal. You are My heart's desire, and I will have you restored into the vision I have held for you since before time. The world's control no longer has the power to shape you; the Cross is the final roadblock. Instead, new creation truths of freedom and innocence bring forth your royal identity.

May 26

Y HEART OPENED A FOUNTAIN. Dive in. Swimming in the fluid of love you are immersed in cleansing blood. Light is dancing and the songs of birds are heard. Newly clothed, step out for you are created to touch the earth in life giving motion. I am in you, more powerful than death. Look My way for I am the rock, more solid than this world. As you move forward darkness gives way.

May 27

YOU ARE A LAMB IN A MEADOW WHERE THE SUN IS FILTERING DOWN THROUGH MAJESTIC WHITE CLOUDS. Kick up your legs and play. Know I am the Shepherd nearby and watch over you. I paid a great price for you and love to see you having a joy filled day. I will lead you down to a clear blue stream where your thirst will be filled. When you are tuckered out, I will lift you up and hold you next to My heart. Allow its rhythm to fill you with peace for you are loved and protected.

May 28

YOU ARE RARE AND EXQUISITE TO ME. I long for you to enter into the appreciation I have of you. Do not waste time with self-demeaning thoughts. Instead renew your mind with the love I have for you. Envision resurrection day where I took you through the Cross to victory. You are the trophy. You are the diamond I gave all for. See yourself through My eyes.

May 29

YOUR NEGATIVE THOUGHTS IN THE MORNING LEAD YOU NOWHERE. See the sunrise as a promise of a new day. Hear the cooing of the dove and know there is opportunity to rejoice. You are not in a pit. In Me there is great expanse to move forward from bare winter branches into springtime blossoms.

May 30

O NOT RETURN EVIL. Look the other way to the Cross. See Me there and know I am a redeemer. Unfairness and cruelty must not flow through one of Mine. Your life is lit by the beauty of love. Do not let the hand of hate cast its shadow within you. Let My resurrection power raise you to a different level, where the world will be confounded and impacted by your choice to forgive.

May 31

RELEASE ALL IN YOUR HEART THAT IS NOT OF ME. I am jealous for your devotion. Listen to My kindness to you that flows continually from the throne room. Harsh and critical words in your mind are not from Me. Like a faucet turn them off and come to the well of living water that will cleanse you making you refreshed. Splash in the waterfall of My joy and all sadness and anxiety must go, especially as you dive into the reality of My love for you. Laughter will break out when you see the freedom I am bringing you to. Come forth and wrap yourself in the robe of righteousness knowing you are pure before My eyes.

66 Fear not, for I have redeemed you; I have called you by your name; you are Mine. When you pass through waters, I will be with you; and through the rivers, they shall not overflow you. When you walk through the fire, you shall not be burned, nor shall the flame scorch you. 99   Isaiah 43:1-2 (NKJV)

June

My roar goes out and
any evil foundation that
has lodged within you
is shattered and blown
away by the breath of
love I have for you.

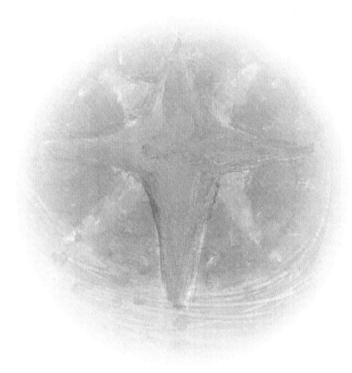

June 1

BELIEVE IN YOUR GREAT VALUE. Neglect by the world and others, as well as your own mistakes and missteps, does not determine your worth. I do. The expanse of creation needed you. You are here because you are My jewel. Shine forth the glory I see and placed within you.

June 2

YOUR SELF-EFFORT TO KEEP RULES IS NOT THE KEY TO UNLOCK HEAVEN. It is your death and resurrection in Me that frees you to enter in. I liberated you from the law that only accentuated your sin. Grace has come. Your life is now hidden in Me. Rest in who I am, and your actions will line up with your righteousness. The pull of sin will lose its attraction.

June 3

LET THE CROSS SPEAK TO YOU WHEN YOU ARE WOUNDED AND SAD. See us joined there. There is no depth I would not go to, just to be with you. Realize My resurrection is yours as well. It is powerful and unstoppable, able to lift you up from the death you feel. As the lamb slain before time, I personally had you in mind to be the answer you need to find hope and life.

June 4

YOUR ACTIONS WILL LINE UP WITH TRUTH AND BEAUTY AS YOU SEE WHAT WAS ACCOMPLISHED BY YOUR DEATH IN ME ON THE CROSS. Sin was defeated and your righteousness was secured. I give you the power to overcome by My faith that saw you before creation as My chosen one. You are not at the mercy of darkness for My light within you is destined to shine brighter and brighter.

June 5

EVERY MORNING, ENJOY THE DEPTHS OF THE COOL CLEAR WATER OF THE WORD. Within it swim into the realization that you are a new creation, free of the realm of dust. Glories of golden splendor surround you as you walk out onto the pristine ground of the Kingdom of Light. The sound of love is heard from the court of your King. Replenishment is there for you before you step forth into your day.

June 6

YOU DO NOT HAVE TO BE AFRAID. I am with you. The Cross shows the extent of My determination to never be separate from you. We have been united in the beauty of resurrection. You have new creation life through Me. Be courageous; the world of pain and disappointment must give way to the true reality of My Kingdom. Love triumphs there. Walk forward with optimism and fear will give way to freedom and joy.

June 7

WHEN YOU FEEL THE CAPTIVITY OF YOUR CIRCUMSTANCES, TURN TO ME. A river of life is flowing from Me. So, refreshment will come. I am larger than your problems and have the answer. Freedom is at hand.

June 8

WALK AMONG OTHERS WITH THE REALIZATION THAT MY LOVE FOR THEM IS ENDLESS. Go with the current of My heart's desire to see each one cherished. You are a conduit for Me to bring good into their lives. See the Cross and know the cost they were to Me and their tremendous value will be revealed to you. You have the privilege to be My messenger. I have entrusted you with the gift of My resurrection life which has the potential to set the captives free.

June 9

I WILL ENDORSE YOU AS YOU STEP OUT INTO YOUR DREAMS. The fear that looms ahead can be punctured and deflated as you take the sword of My word and wield it defensively. The richness of who you are exceeds the poverty you feel. The wealth of heaven is on your side and the entrance of faith and grace will lead you to the domain where all things are possible.

June 10

YOU ARE NEVER IGNORED BY ME. People may pass you by, but I do not. I have made a great investment in you. The Cross reflects that. The world is a shaky foundation; identifying with it will only weaken you. Look to Me. Only I supply what is necessary. My love is the strongest force in the universe. Enter into its flow to find your strength.

June 11

I **AM THE FIRE WITHIN YOU BURNING TO MAKE YOUR LIFE RADIANT.** You are alive by the flames of My love that reflect brilliant light upon you. Be the warmth of My affection to everyone you meet. Brighten their world with My light. The heat of My love through you can warm cold hearts that have been lost within the darkness.

June 12

YOU ARE NEARER TO ME THAN YOU KNOW. Rest in our oneness. I paid a great price for the union we share. Sense My life in you that undergirds you to flourish. Step out in the joy I have of you. You were preplanned before creation. Now you are here to come into the destiny prepared for you.

June 13

AM PROTECTIVE OVER YOU BECAUSE YOU ARE MY HEART'S DESIRE. You are safe to be who you are with Me. I will never judge you less than. Move forward, dropping all that does not match your true identity. Your potential was something I guaranteed before creation. Your destiny shines like the sun for we are joined together and in Me there is no darkness.

June 14

YOUR INPUT TO THOSE AROUND YOU IS VALUABLE. Take the time to care. Always listen to My agenda and be willing to lay yours down. The broken-hearted take precedence over your rise to the top. Tunnel vision on yourself blocks the beautiful path I lay before you. Know that true success is a life of love.

June 15

MY LOVE FOR YOU CANNOT BE ALTERED. The Cross is a seal that shows the extent of what I would go through for you. Clear away the thoughts in your mind that would separate you from Me. I am here and I do not move. I am the rock on which to build your life. All else is sinking sand.

June 16

~

YOUR PLACE IN THE WORLD IS NOT AS IMPORTANT AS THE PLACE YOU HAVE IN MY HEART. My love is never fleeting. You can rely on the unchanging nature of who I am. Worldly positions shift like sand, but I am a solid foundation. Set your focus on Me alone and your life will unfold into marvelous dimensions that far exceed the shallow waters of the worldly system.

June 17

OIN ME IN THE LOVE I HAVE FOR
OTHERS. Your kindness to those around
you is highly valued by Me. As you reach out, I
am always with you. Draw upon the heart I have
for each person. See through My eyes the quality
I am crafting and call that forth. My light is
meant to shine through you.

June 18

THE HARSH TONE YOU LISTEN TO IS NOT MINE. Stop giving yourself to lies that disfigure who I paid for you to be. Any harmful ugly thought toward yourself or anyone else is not from Me. Remember all failure and disgrace were nailed with Me at the Cross. The sin of the world was on Me and the victory I accomplished there was to set you free. Tune into My loving voice; allow it to be the theme of your life.

June 19

THE HARD TIME YOU ARE IN IS PAINTING YOUR LIFE WITH GOLD, SO NEVER DESPAIR. Believe in My goodness that marks the Kingdom in which you are a citizen. Nothing is wasted there. Lift your sight to the Cross where I declared My love for you. See also the resurrection as My promise. Truly daylight comes after the darkness of night.

June 20

RIGHTEOUSNESS SHINES FORTH IN YOU, A GIFT FROM ME. Be strong in the fact that you are Mine and are made new. You have been lifted up to share seating with Me above life's circumstances. Your steps are ordered to bring forth a harvest of fruit. Stand firm in the love that is covering you as a heavenly blanket. You are secure at all times. Nothing of darkness can penetrate. You are priceless to Me.

June 21

AS AN EAGLE SOARS IN THE SKY ALLOW YOUR HEART TO SOAR WITHIN THE LOVE THAT IS COMING TO YOU FROM ON HIGH. It is powerful to lift you from all circumstances that would come against you. You are called to focus on the heavenly heights where love and light prevail.

June 22

Nothing can withstand My love. Hard circumstances in the earthly realm have no strength against Me. I am reigning throughout all eternity. I have chosen you. With and within you I will prevail. Golden veins of light shine in you as you are a new creation. Hold on in confidence that you are a pearl of great price to Me and I will never let you go.

June 23

*I*N THE LOVE THAT IS STRONGER THAN DEATH I ABIDE AND DWELL WHERE YOU ARE. The strength of that love can fortify you against fears that would assail. Thanksgiving and praise that you are secured in My heart can fend off danger. Rejoice for I have chosen to indwell you and My power for your good has no limits.

June 24

❧

YOU ARE ONE STEP FROM THE THRONE ROOM AT ANY TIME. When the day seems oppressive and hard, enter in. You are most welcome. You will be received with great love and attention. The world may shun you, but I desire your presence and delight when you come My way.

June 25

BE STILL AND KNOW THAT BEFORE THE EARTH WAS FORMED YOU WERE IN MY HEART. Your day was anticipated. Love called you forth into a Kingdom whose entrance was the Cross. Your old life was done away with and a new resurrected one is yours. Delight in Me whose dream you are, for I have made only good for you.

June 26

RAW YOUR SATISFACTION FROM ME ALONE. Do not go to other places for your fulfillment. I have what you need. My heart is immense for you. It has invigorating properties that will cause you to thrive as you explore its depths. You will become a carrier of My love as you fasten all that you are to Me. Lives around you will feel the impact of who I am through you. You will be a vessel of My love and light.

June 27

THE GREAT ADVENTURE OF KNOWING
ME IS ENDLESS. The largeness of who
I am can never be fully explored. Come catch the
excitement. I have called you out of darkness into a
Kingdom of Light that will never end. I am here to
enable you to accomplish great feats. With Me all
things are possible.

June 28

ENDEAVOR TO HOLD ME IN YOUR HEART AT ALL TIMES. You will be secured into Godly strength as you do. I will empower you to live in a Kingdom reality where light shines upon your way. You will triumph over the world's attempts to lure you for you will see My life as the true wealth.

June 29

MY FIRE BURNS BRIGHT TO BRING CLARITY OF WHAT IS REAL AND LASTING. It will take care of impediments that keep you on the sideline of your own life. Come in and become a burning one for Me. My love is red hot for My created ones. You too must radiate love for I have called you into My heart to blaze for Me.

June 30

Y OU HAVE A UNIQUE EXPRESSION OF WHO I AM IN YOU. Be brave to show it forth. Take steps toward your destiny for the Cross broke the barrier that kept you enclosed. Sin can no longer stop you from freely advancing with the resources of My Kingdom at your side.

" But whoever drinks of the water that I shall give him will never thirst. But the water that I shall give him will become in him a fountain of water springing up into everlasting life. "

John 4:14 (NKJV)

July

When the heat of the sun
beats down and times seem
tough, come with Me to the
river of living water that flows
continually. Dive in and let
Me take you on a joyous ride
as we share laughter together.

July 1

YOU ARE NEVER OUTSIDE OF My SPHERE. My love supersedes any hint of separation for we have been joined together by My desire. On the Cross all that keeps you out was abolished. Never feel forsaken or abandoned. Instead, see Me close to you at all times. The price I paid for you shows how dear you are to Me.

July 2

MY LOVE FOR YOU IS WRITTEN OUT IN BLOOD. It poured down into a darkened world and brought great light of redemption for you. You are cleansed and made new by My sacrifice. It gave Me pleasure to rescue you. So set your mind on the infinite price I paid to have you and know your value. Do not undercut in any way who you are. You are My betrothed and My desire.

July 3

ELOW THE STARS ON A WARM SUMMER NIGHT, THE GENTLE BREEZE BLOWING, ENVISION YOURSELF AS A MAJOR PART IN MY HEART. Draw from the sense of importance I place on you. The cosmos needed your reflection of Me.

July 4

STAY THE COURSE. You are in Me and I am in you no matter how you feel. Acknowledge that fact when you do not see it and it will become real again. I never leave you. Look at the Cross, at the depths of where I would go to be with you. I understand the hard experience you face. I will get you through for truly My victory on resurrection day is yours. Persevere and it will manifest in your life.

July 5

YOUR LOVE IS POWERFUL. It has the ability to break the chains of those around you. Your care, concern, and kindness can move mountains for the needy in your life. Be alert and listen to the beat of My heart. It will guide you in this most important endeavor.

July 6

WHEN YOUR MIND IS PAINFULLY RACING REALIZE I AM HERE. Turn away from your frantic flight response. Slow down and quiet yourself with Me. Take time to tune into My heart. I will direct you in love to take the steps that are needed. Even if you stay here with Me you are accomplishing a lot. I fill you with all that is necessary as you drink in the empowering love I have for you.

July 7

MY LOVE FOR YOU IS A STRONG FORCE. Utilize it to strengthen your life. Do not waste time seeking the world's approval when it is My approval that frees you. As you focus on the importance you are to Me and allow it to penetrate your awareness, you will become emboldened to flourish.

July 8

I **HAVE PROVIDED A LIFE OF LIGHT.** On the Cross you were cut away from the cord of darkness as I drew all sin into Myself and overcame death. Believe the crucifixion set you free. Resurrection is your portion. Circumstances will bend to the victory achieved there. Patiently persevere and this truth will become your reality.

July 9

WHEN YOU HELP TO LIFT THE BURDEN OF ANOTHER IT DELIGHTS MY HEART. The light in your action shines eternally and is no small thing in heaven's sight. The world may think you foolish. But know I am behind you and within you. You reflect My wisdom which is deeper, purer, and more beautiful.

July 10

YOU ARE LOVED NO MATTER THE DEPTH TO WHICH YOU PLUNGE. I am here and provide a path of recovery. Know that condemnation does not originate from Me. Do not look at your accusers' faces; see only Mine. Listen and wait for golden encouragement that is coming your way. I am in you and cradle you in My heart. In time transformation will come.

July 11

YOUR KINDNESS IS THE STRONGEST THING ABOUT YOU. It can break the bonds of sorrow that grip another. It can melt a stone-cold heart. It can light a fire of confidence in a timid soul. Never measure your strength by how brash and self-important you are but in how you treat your fellow sojourners. Partner with Me and who I am in you, then tap into the powerful ancient source of the Golden Rule.

July 12

YOUR GOOD WORD TO OTHERS HAS SUBSTANCE THAT SOLIDIFIES INTO GOLD AS YOU ARE TRUE AND FAITHFUL TO IT. The world's way shifts like sand. But in the Kingdom there is a foundation of truth that resonates in its citizens. My character is faithful; reflect who I am in you.

July 13

Y AFFECTION FOR YOU IS MORE REAL THAN ANY ISOLATED AND ALONE EXISTENCE YOU PERCEIVE. My love gives you your next breath. I sustain you daily. I foresaw you eons ago and rejoice that you are alive here and now. Enjoy My delight of you and see yourself for the gift you are.

July 14

YOU ARE SECURE IN MY HEART. You will never slip away by missteps or neglect. I am here at all points. Just return to the awareness of My love when you have ventured down foolish paths. The redemption of the Cross always stands.

July 15

LET THE LOVE I HAVE FOR YOU MOVE YOU FORWARD FROM THE PAIN OF REJECTION YOU HAVE RECEIVED IN THE WORLD. The truth is My desire of you is full of fire that lights a path of victory for you to walk in. Warm yourself in My love and the cold stares that controlled your life will melt into the past. The future spills out with promise under My loving gaze. Delight yourself in My delight of you and you will meet obstacles that seemed formidable before and will go right through them.

July 16

YOU MATTER. Your life is a story to be told. Embrace the importance of who you are to Me. Rely on My acceptance as you venture out where your heart leads. My belief in you was strong enough to bring you into creation. Allow the platform of My love to propel you forward into the beauty of your existence.

July 17

IFE IS NOT FAIR BUT I AM. The Cross speaks into the places you find yourself surrounded by the agony of darkness. I am acquainted with pain and despair and solidly identify with where you are. My connection to you is real and can ease your situation as you rest in the cushion of My compassion. Know the light of resurrection is ahead.

July 18

TUNE IN AND LISTEN FOR ME. I am easily found. The kindest voice is Mine. Condemning harsh voices are not of Me. Do not allow them to paint My portrait. Do not allow them to paint your portrait either. Instead let My true words of love, favor, and mercy color you with life and freedom.

July 19

DO NOT MEASURE YOUR LIFE BY THOSE AROUND YOU. You are Mine. I qualify you to be the expression of who you are. I say your life echoes unique beauty from My heart. Quit looking to the left or the right for affirmation. Look only to Me to find your value and realize the infinite love I have for you fills the universe.

July 20

IN THE KALEIDOSCOPE OF LIFE, YOU GIVE BEAUTY TO THE PATTERN WITH EACH STEP YOU TAKE. I have united Myself with you and our destinies are entwined. There is glory ahead no matter the darkness you perceive at the moment. Trust Me in you to burst new colors into brilliant light.

July 21

REPLENISHMENT IS IN THE POWERFUL WATER OF THE WORD. Come drink and know invincible life is being poured into you. So supplied, you can face the adverse situations of your day. Nothing outlasts the truth that you are a chosen vessel containing everlasting truth that will quench the short-lived lies from the temporal realm.

July 22

THIS NEW LIFE PAST THE CROSS IS POWERFUL. You have ascended. The pull of the world cannot control you. Love is your force now and in union with Me you can impact those around you for good. Each day is a shining gift. I formed you and am leading you into the glorious depths of the truth the world desperately needs, and which I created you to be able to give.

July 23

IN THE WORLD YOU ARE CALLED TO WALK, BUT YOU ARE NOT OF IT. The troubles therein cannot overcome you as you remember the Kingdom of Light is within your heart and is your true home. Its domain is a safe place to be. I am a righteous King there. My eye is always upon you and My force is behind you as you navigate your day.

July 24

FOREVER YOU ARE HELD IN **M**Y HEART. You can never step outside of My love. Know that wherever you are, I am. You can manage your day realizing that you are united to the One who formed creation with you in mind. Take the tasks before you with confidence for all things are possible in Me.

July 25

MY LONGING IS FOR YOU TO APPLY THE CROSS TO SITUATIONS THAT HINDER AND BRING FEAR TO YOU. Focus on the fact that at the Cross there was a transfer that exchanged death for life. You are not at the mercy of sin and darkness. Their power has been deprived and can no longer control you. Take the freedom My blood delivered to you. See yourself as a new creation endowed with My love, full of beautiful possibilities to receive blessings and to be a blessing.

July 26

MY LOVE OUTLASTS ANY FEAR THAT WOULD COME UPON YOU. Courage comes when you look to Me as your true source. Earthly circumstances fall by the wayside before the Kingdom of light that eternally stands. You are not of the world.

July 27

THE ROOSTER, IN BRILLIANT COLOR, SOUNDS OUT THE MORNING; A NEW DAY IN YOUR HEART HAS COME. I am a great and mighty King and I have risen for you and you arose with Me. Have expectancy as you advance forward. Wonderful things are afoot; let love be your motivation in the Kingdom that is founded on it. The world of darkness cannot encroach. It cringes back from the light whose expanse will never end.

July 28

YOU HAVE BEEN CALLED TO A NEW ORDER WHERE SIN HAS NO LEGAL SAY. I bought you with My life. Believe this and let it propel you through this world. Darkness has some authority in the earthly realm, but not in you, as the indestructible one abides within.

July 29

YOU ARE ACCEPTED BY ME. I see in you a beautiful design and will be faithful to bring it forth. Do not rely on the fickle praise of man or your own self-strivings to uphold you. Instead depend only on Me. I supply what you need. My eternal unbreakable love is powerful to transform any insecurity. When you receive the fact that you are secured in My heart, you will become the victor I have destined you to be.

July 30

MY LOVE BURSTS FOR YOU IN THE SUN THAT COMES UP SHINING OVER THE HORIZON. Each day is My gift to you. Rejoice in the morning birdsong that echoes eternal chords of the joy you bring to Me. My delight is in you. Learn to discern that, My beautiful created one.

July 31

I AM MORE THAN ENOUGH. Do not let thoughts of insufficiencies accost you. You have the power to say no and look only to Me. You are royalty and need to see yourself as such. You are not a slave to circumstances that try to close you in. I am a broad open place full of beauty and wonder. Dwell in Me. Step out of the box you perceive yourself to be in. Remember all things are possible in Me and it is up to you to heed My voice. I say you are Mine and I favor and bless those that belong to Me. So, pull yourself up to the truth of who you are in Me.

"When I consider Your heavens, the work of Your fingers, the moon and the stars, which You have set in place; what is man that You think of him, and a son of man that You are concerned about him? Yet You have made him a little lower than God, and You crown him with glory and majesty! You have him rule over the works of Your hands; You have put everything under his feet."

Psalm 8:3-6 (NASB)

August

At the end of a long day
lean against Me and see the
glory of a golden sunset with
shades of pink and purple. I
painted that there for you. I
am the artist of your life too.

August 1

NEVER FEEL UNDERVALUED. I overcame death with you in mind. Your life was worth the Cross. Realize the depth of My accomplishment there for you. Sin's rule was severed from you and you arose with Me to a new reality. Embrace My victory into your heart. You are My beloved and I equip you to rule and reign.

August 2

ALLOW MY WAVE TO COME UPON THE SHORE OF YOUR HEART TO WASH AWAY ALL DEBRIS THAT DOES NOT LINE UP WITH MY LOVE FOR YOU. Then collect the beautiful shells left that reveal My intent. They are glistening truths that say you are worthy and Holy before Me. Breathe in the fresh air and soak in the sunlight as you carry your treasures. Let them remind you that you are My treasure.

August 3

I F YOU ARE CAUGHT IN A BAD HABIT
DO NOT LOOK TO THE LAW TO RESCUE
YOU. Instead, focus on the fact that I am within
you. My incorruptible love is powerful to unlock
the patterns that have kept you bound. As you
become aware that you are the desire of My heart,
the flame of My love will begin to enlighten your
life. Darkness will flee for I truly came to set the
captive free.

August 4

YOU CANNOT ESCAPE MY LOVE. It is here for you at all times. You may disappoint yourself and lay in the dust. But I have cleansed you by My blood. You are new in Me. Pick yourself up and declare the truth of your righteousness that I paid for. Lift your head and move forward. Realize you have great hope and security in who I am in you.

August 5

HEN YOU FEEL ALONE REMEMBER I AM HERE. I went to great lengths to have you with Me. The Cross did away with all separation. Your company is what I desired. So, look to Me to fill the ache in your heart. Others may come and go but I remain with you always. Know that the thought of you has delighted Me since before the cosmos was formed. You are never unwanted by Me.

August 6

YOUR FAMILY CAN BE A CRUCIBLE. Mother, father, sister, brother, daughter, son can pour on the coals. Know we are there together. As you bear it with grace, in time, purified, you will come forth as gold and the ash will blow away. You will be the shining one and your family can enter a new day.

August 7

SILENCE THE INSECURITIES THAT EXALT THE OLD ADAMIC MAN ABOVE ME. Do not run with them anymore. They are deceitful lovers that take you away from Me. I am jealous for you and call you to a higher place of commitment to Me. This is the day to turn to Me completely. I am the mighty God who laid the foundation of creation. I spoke all into existence. What I say about you stands forever. You are cleansed by costly blood. You have been made new and secured into My Kingdom as royalty. Enter into your position. Die to what was crucified in Me. Allow resurrection life to come forth. The fact that I am with you is enough.

August 8

YOU WERE ENVISIONED IN ME BEFORE YOU WERE FORMED. Set your sights on the sight I had on you. Rejoice for I sing over you with joy. In Me you have been raised to a new beginning. All that impeded you of sin was done away with on the Cross where I took you into My death to truly set you free.

August 9

ALLOW MY LOVE TO BE A FLAME TO BURN AWAY THE UNKIND WORDS OR ACTIONS OF OTHERS. Let My favor over you liberate you from accusation and slander that imprisons. Step out into the freedom I provide. See in your mind the high worth you have in My economy, where the Cross stands eternally as the message of your value.

August 10

WHEN THE WORLD AND PEOPLE ARE CUTTING AT TIMES KNOW THAT MY BLOOD FELL DOWN FOR YOU. As you hurt, I am there with you in the experience. The Cross is My statement of love for you. You were joined to Me there and I took you from the grave into resurrection life. Breathe the air of your redemption. Be filled with the truth that nothing can stain you. Lock your heart with Mine. Be fortified by My passion for you. You are My desire, and I will be your vindication. Trust in Me.

August 11

YOUR STRIVINGS TO FEEL IMPORTANT ARE NOT NEEDED. I see your value. You shine in My heart like the stars above. Rest in My favor of you. Sink into My acceptance and relinquish the fear that you are not good enough. I am pleased that you are Mine. Allow My pleasure of you to set you free.

August 12

THE CONDEMNATION YOU FEEL IS NOT FROM ME. You do not have to earn My favor. I have called you into being for My delight. Center your thoughts on Me and My view of you. Take your eyes off yourself and your perceived failure and lack. I have abundance for you. My love is immense. Allow it to empower your life. As you do you will find peace and fulfillment.

August 13

I WANT YOU TO BE GOOD BUT REALIZE YOUR GOODNESS COMES FROM YOUR IDENTITY IN ME. Rest in the fact that we have been united at the Cross and rose together to be eternally joined. Look to Me to see who you truly are. Our relationship enables you to act with a kind heart far more than a code of right and wrong does. Realization of My loving embrace allows you to lovingly embrace others.

August 14

WHEN YOU HAVE BEEN BORN FROM ABOVE, THE LIGHT OF GRACE SHINES CLEARLY TO LEAD YOU INTO FREEDOM. The crushing weight of the law has been set aside and your captivity has ended. Sin's domination is no longer. With confidence know the new covenant has radically delivered you into a lasting union with Me. Now you have a living way written in your heart that enables you to walk in the power of My transforming love.

August 15

MY LIQUID LOVE IN THE FORM OF HOLY BLOOD WAS SPILT FOR YOU. Be resilient in the fact that you have been made clean, washed by the wonder of it. Contamination from sin is no longer the issue. This resounding truth must pervade your life, allowing you to freely walk into deeper revelation of who I am.

August 16

OUR IMPORTANCE IS SECURE IN ME. I see your value. Your efforts for self-approval and recognition are backwards. Allow My approval of you to propel you forward. My acceptance liberates you from the treadmill of performance orientation. A genuine life of peace and joy will arise as you connect to My vision of you and relinquish fragmented worldly images that kept you bound.

August 17

G LISTENING WITH POWER THE WORD
COMES TO REFINE YOU. Unraveling
behind you are fears and worries as I am the rock,
solid and true, that holds you up in the brightness
of My life. Grace hums beautiful songs of freedom
where you can walk on water and see what has
not been seen, that you shine as a new creation
sparkling with My love. The storm may come
but within you the Word is more real than all the
darkness. You are free to believe My goodness for I
poured out blood to wash you clean eternally.

August 18

YOU HAVE BEEN BIRTHED INTO A LIGHT FILLED KINGDOM. Your residence there allows you to go about your day with a higher perspective. The world will press in, but your life is hidden safely away in Me. Our union allows you to face adversity with confidence. I am in control and you are in safe hands.

August 19

YOUR OLD LIFE HAS BEEN REPLACED NO MATTER WHAT IT FEELS LIKE. You are now royalty and of a new race. You have been put in My lineage and have a great inheritance. Walk with your head raised. Love has pulled you from the mire of sin and now you are righteous. Joy is your new strength when you see the immensity of what has been done for you.

August 20

DRINK IN THE LOVE I HAVE FOR YOU AND PARCHED LAND WILL BEGIN TO BLOSSOM. The Cross is a love letter that did away with sin's power to scorch you. You have been made pristine by My blood. See yourself as I see you. You are pure and beautiful in My sight.

August 21

PULL YOURSELF UP TO THE IMAGE I HAVE OF YOU. Refuse old voices that say you are unworthy. You are worth Holy blood, Mine, that has set you free. Quit allowing thoughts that prod you into corners of fear, stagnation, and regret. The gate is wide open. Come to Me, the Shepherd of your soul. I will allow you to lie down in green pastures with warm sunshine and a bubbling brook nearby. All is well if you look only to Me. Those nipping accusers have no strength before Me. They were disarmed at the Cross so do not allow them to intimidate you. Now rise in peace and go forward knowing I am within you.

261

August 22

YOU CAN BE NO CLOSER THAN YOU ARE TO ME. I reside within you. Take heart I am here. Rely on Me as you navigate your day. When things look bad, breathe in My love, and know I paid a high price to be close to you. I will see you through.

August 23

*I*F YOU HAVE BEEN HATEFUL TO OTHERS COME TO ME. There is a torn place in your heart that I can mend. You can come out from the heaviness of loathing. Peer into the daylight of love that I shine for you. The dank dark room of bitterness is no place for one of Mine. Take the key of forgiveness I offer and see there is a glorious life beyond the stale shadows and cobwebs you embraced.

August 24

THE KNOT OF SIN THAT ENTANGLES YOU
IS NO MATCH TO THE STRENGTH OF MY
LOVE. Look away from your failure to My success
on the Cross. The empty tomb is your reality.
Come out with Me to a new day. Resurrection frees
you from any chain of bad decisions you have made
and sets you on a path to victorious redemption.

August 25

THE CROSS IS A DOORWAY OF MY LOVE FOR YOU. The harm of this world can never take away the redemption I provided. My arrival on earth signified My intent to close all distance. My nearness to you is closer than your breath. Come out of any loneliness or alienation and rejoice that we are eternally joined.

August 26

THE SMALL AREA YOU EXIST IN BECOMES LARGER WHEN YOU EXTEND YOUR HEART FOR ANOTHER. The shallow ground of self-centeredness and self-gratification give way to the depth of eternal love that extends to all people. The contacts you touch with the beauty of kindness and consideration become ignited; a chain of light is set in motion and the world is a less dark place.

August 27

YOU HAVE BEEN CALLED INTO ROYALTY.
I paved the way by My blood to welcome
you into Kingdom life.   I have given you My mind.
Do not allow bad thoughts to enslave you ever again.
All things are possible if you believe and align with Me.
Love painted you in My heart before creation; now you
are the living embodiment of My dream. Know that
you are dearly loved and were greatly anticipated. Your
life is of much value to Me. Therefore, move through
your day with confidence knowing you are equipped
to face whatever comes. Your circumstances can shine
with My life as you rest in My goodness and know I
am the peace in any storm.

August 28

YOU ARE NOT AN AFTERTHOUGHT. You are the purpose I cherished in My heart before time. Your existence is My joy. My radiance is within you and we are linked eternally. Nourish yourself with My love that is sustaining you at all times.

August 29

THE DARK NIGHT IN YOUR SOUL WILL BECOME A MEMORY THAT WILL GIVE BEAUTIFUL DIMENSION TO YOUR LIFE. The gold veins left behind will provide riches to others in mourning that come your way from time to time. You will be a supplier of heartfelt knowing and understanding that is often hard to find in this world.

August 30

WHEN YOU ARE TORN FROM BETRAYAL AND ACCUSATION AND FEEL THE DEATH OF THAT PAIN, SEE ME ON THE CROSS AND KNOW I AM JOINED WITH YOU. I hear further than your heart can cry. Come to Me and let Me gather you in a resurrection blanket and lift you from the tomb into the light of a new day.

August 31

THE FIERCENESS OF MY LOVE IS REAL. There is nothing that can keep Me away from you. I removed it all at the Cross. You may be unaware of My attention for you, but I have you in My heart at all times. Relinquish anything in you that clouds sight of that. Look only to Me as your source. I alone have what you need. I designed you for Me. Only I can complete you. As you die to what distracts you, you will come alive in Me. My righteousness paints you in light. The shadows can no longer dictate. I am the One to listen to now. In Me you will find the strength to be who I call you to be.

" But this I call to mind, and therefore I have hope: The steadfast love of the Lord never ceases; His mercies never come to an end; they are new every morning; great is Your faithfulness. "

Lamentations 3:21-23 (ESV)

September

When weariness is upon
you curl up next to Me.
Feel My warmth. Hear
My steady heartbeat and
let it infuse you with
new strength. Renewal
will come.

September 1

CCESS HAS BEEN GRANTED TO YOU THROUGH THE CROSS INTO A KINGDOM OF LIGHT. Do not be deterred by dark and hard conditions in the natural. Be arrested by My love that never stops flowing to you from My resoluteness that paid for you in blood. You are capable in My capabilities. I will enable you to walk out the call into the divine destiny you were created for.

September 2

I DO NOT LOVE YOU FOR WHAT YOU CAN ACCOMPLISH. You are My accomplishment. I saw you in My heart before creation. I entered human life to reclaim you as Mine from a fallen life of distortion. I achieved your redemption. Come into My approval of you and rest. From that place of quiet acceptance move out with who I am in you. Let your inner strivings subside as My strength arises to reign in your life.

September 3

ONLY YOU CAN RELEASE THE IDEA THAT YOU DO NOT MEASURE UP. I declared on the Cross your worth. Do not retreat to a small place of perceived insignificance when I provide a rich open expanse and a royal life for you to live. Set yourself free from constricted thoughts of failure as I have given you My mind that declares you victorious.

September 4

RAW FROM MY AFFECTION FOR YOU. Allow it to do away with your self-unacceptance. The Cross is My statement to you. Let My blood wash away the lies that say you are unworthy. I declared you a treasure that gladly cost My own life. Your richness is a reality. The quality I see in you is radiant; allow it to shine forth leaning on the strength of My love.

September 5

THIS HARD SHELL AROUND YOU CAN BE CRACKED OPEN. Push against the idea that says I harshly judge. Come out into the amazement I have of you. I see you beautiful and worthy of expression. Be unafraid to break through and the life I paid for in blood for you will manifest in the preordained glory that is yours as a gift.

September 6

I **CREATED YOU WITH A BEAUTIFUL VISION.** The Cross was the place that annihilated all that marred you. Come into the wholeness I provided. Lay down anger, bitterness, and jealousy. Pick up the blanket of affection I have for you. Wrap up and fall into the comfort of true love that values you beyond behavior. You are Mine regardless. Come to Me with your wounds. I will be your healing. The Cross opened a river that will cleanse and restore you to the image I have of you. You are My delight and always have been.

September 7

LOOK AWAY FROM YOUR SIN TO ME. I am capable to transform you as you focus on what was done for you at the Cross. The darkness gave way to resurrection light. Your placement in Me is secured by My love. Love is stronger than death. There is no trap that I have not opened for you. Come out into the purity I paid for you to have. You are cleansed by My blood and I see you worthy. Surrender old patterns that tell otherwise.

September 8

SEE BEYOND THE NARROW CONFINES OF A RELIGIOUS SYSTEM THAT HAS YOU CONSTANTLY WORKING FOR APPROVAL. Your work is to believe that the Cross severed you from the crushing weight of the law. The new covenant operates in a radically different way. Within it you have received My spirit that leads you to rest. My satisfaction in My accomplishment that imparted righteousness to you must become yours. Receive My acceptance and let My love be your driving force.

September 9

FEAR IS AN INTRUDER. It does not belong with you like a dear friend does. Turn it out. Instead realize I am here to be your true companion. My goodness is far beyond the crippling lies that fear has continuously whispered. Lean into My voice that will fortify you with the truth that I have your back. You can rely on Me. Before creation I saw you and declared your life was necessary for Me. You are here because of My love. I will see to your needs, concerns, and desires.

September 10

YOU HAVE BEEN EXQUISITELY MADE TO REFLECT MY LIGHT. No one can be who I have made you to be. Darkness will try to cast its shadow on your life but it is powerless against My vision for you. Rise up into the destiny that you are called to. Come out from the vestiges of your old existence. Leave them behind forever. Truly new creation realities sparkle from within you. My life and love empower you to encounter each situation with victory.

September 11

THE STRAIN YOU LIVE UNDER TO PROVE YOURSELF VALUABLE MUST GIVE WAY TO THE PEACE OF WHO I AM IN YOU. Rest in Me. There is no price tag for My love. You do not have to earn your way into My heart. I have joined you to Me by way of the Cross because you were that important to Me. Sense our union and the pressure to attain something you already have will subside. You are released to be free and show forth the beautiful new creation I formed you to be.

September 12

THE GATE OF THE KINGDOM IS OPENED TO YOU. You have been called to walk through with royal authority. The world in which you live must succumb to My ways there. Listen to My commands. Decree forth My light and love and manifestation of My glory will triumph in the earthly realm.

September 13

AR INTO THE PAST BEFORE CREATION
I SAW YOU. I destined you for this day.
Nothing you could do could keep Me from the love
I have for you. I embraced you into Myself when I
endured the Cross so you would not be under sin's
control. Lift your head up and look to Me and you
will be transformed into My vision of you.

September 14

WHEN YOU FEEL REJECTED AND ALONE, KNOW THE PRICE OF THE CROSS I PAID TO HAVE YOU. Your companionship is what I desired from the beginning. I am here to be your friend and you can depend on Me. Listen for the kind words I whisper and believe them in your heart and My love will unfold before you.

September 15

NEGATIVE THINKING CAN BLOCK YOUR DESTINY. Critical and biting thoughts about yourself and others go against Me. I went to the Cross for the beautiful value I saw in you all. To disregard this action of love for the seductive lies of the accuser is dangerous and causes damage. I call you to a higher level and equip and enable you to change as you look to Me. I am the key that will unlock the dark patterns you have embraced.

September 16

RAW FROM THE FOUNTAIN OF MY LOVE AND QUENCH YOUR THIRST; THEN TAKE THE BUCKET OF YOUR LIFE AND POUR IT OUT TO OTHERS. A parched world is in need of the life-giving properties I placed within you. Look around and see the dry areas where material and spiritual poverty abound. Go forth leaving a trail of flowers behind you.

September 17

WHEN YOU ARE FEELING DISABLED BY WORLDLY CARES AND WOES, STOP AND REALIZE WHO MAINTAINS YOUR LIFE. You are in complete union with Me. Reset your focus on My accomplishment for you. I was the victor over sin and have set you in a heavenly position. Rely on the truth that you exist above, and negative earthly circumstances will loosen their hold and you will begin to excel in My love and light.

September 18

I LOVE YOU. Remember to only tune into what I say. Pay attention to My love all day. Draw your identity from Me at all times. Only have ears for My voice. I am jealous for you. Do not let the lesser things cloud your mind. Put all that you are in My care. Your concerns matter to Me. I will iron them out in time, all will be made well. Keep coming to Me and enjoy Me. Let the inferior things fall away. I am your target; aim for Me with all that you are and I will richly provide for you.

September 19

Y OU ARE BEAUTIFUL TO ME. I crafted you in My heart before the world was formed. I destined you to be Mine. Do not fear what the day may hold for I have united Myself to you by way of the Cross. All that tied you to darkness has been cut off. You are in the light as I am. Let the truth of My goodness transform you. Breathe in the freedom that is yours through Me.

September 20

~

THE WIND AND THE WAVES CONTINUE TO MOVE, AND I TOO AM WORKING WITHIN YOU IN A CONSTANT MANNER. You are My concern and all you put your hand to is worked into My plan for you. At every point I am with you so rest and enjoy the ride of life I have provided. It is a gift given with great care; navigate with confidence.

September 21

YOU CAN FLY. I have given you wings. I see you soaring. The horizon is before you and possibilities are endless. Love, the strongest force, is within you. Tap into it and catch the wind of My Spirit. Enjoy the movement of a resurrected and ascended life.

September 22

WHEN THE CLOUD OF CONCERNS CLOSES IN, KNOW THE SUNLIGHT OF WHO I AM WILL BREAK THROUGH. Hold fast to the hope you have in Me and the blanket of darkness will dissipate, and you will see golden solutions shine.

September 23

KNOW THAT GRATITUDE WILL SPILL LIKE HONEY INTO YOUR HEART MAKING LIFE SWEET. See your blessings and focus on their goodness. Let the hard and bitter things have no preeminence in your mind. Instead bask in the light that filters through to you each day. Realize My provision for your contentment is in your reach.

September 24

KINDNESS AND CONSIDERATION ARE PRICELESS COMMODITIES THAT BRING ENRICHMENT TO YOU AS YOU ENGAGE THEM. Your thoughtfulness of others draws abundance to your own existence. Any behavior less than only takes away and diminishes. Do not waste time with selfish and uncharitable actions that impede the goodness life can be. Your choices make a difference. Choose wisely.

September 25

HEN YOU WERE TORN AWAY FROM ME AT THE FALL I HAD ALREADY BLED AS THE LAMB SLAIN. The journey to the Cross was worth the victory I won to have you back. Love is the strongest force and death had lost all options. See the glorious story unfold with your part gleaming as a precious stone sewn into a beautiful tapestry.

September 26

ALLOW THE WIND OF THE SPIRIT TO BLOW AWAY ANY LIES THAT SAY YOU ARE NOT WORTHY. You have been spoken for by Me. I selected you as My own. Realize My approval is upon you. You have been brought into My Kingdom and made royal. Your union with Me makes you glorious.

September 27

AM WITHIN YOU. You do not have to go anywhere or earn anything to enter My presence. Be still and let the breath you take remind you of My constant love and that I am attentive to your life.

September 28

I AM HERE WITH YOU. You are not your own. I have bought you with My own blood. You are priceless to Me. Untie your anxious heart and place it into My hand. This day is Mine, and I will see you through. Hear what I say and turn your ear away from any voice that is not Mine. Do not welcome the tormenter by opening the door. Keep it shut and stay in the special place with Me; in My Kingdom room that surrounds you with light and luxury. It is a place of rest. Lean against Me in a relaxed pose. In this place of togetherness listen to My instruction; I will tell you what to do.

September 29

BE LIFTED UP FROM THE SHADOWS OF NEGATIVE THOUGHTS. Fill yourself with the beauty of who I say you are. My blood paid for your righteousness. You are cleansed and made new and have been joined to Me in a perfect union. Rest in our oneness. Allow My peace to rule. Receive the vastness of My love and it will propel your life.

September 30

ANY KINDNESS NO MATTER HOW SMALL DOES NOT GO UNNOTICED. You are celebrated in My heart as you walk out My character. You were born to be a recipient of My love and a vehicle of the love I give. I support the efforts you take to shine a light into another's darkness. Know the force of heaven is on your side as you do and applauds the difference you make.

> 66 *For the creation waits in eager expectation for the children of God to be revealed.* 99

Romans 8:19 (NIV)

October

Billowing clouds against a blue sky; underneath a field of gold. Walk with Me and I will show you beauty within and without. Creation smiles upon you because you are My child.

October 1

YOU ARE NOT MADE FOR LESS THAN I SEE YOU TO BE. My love is a beautifying force. Receive it into your innermost being. As you connect to My view of you, you will be elevated to new levels. The expansiveness of My heart for you will expand your life in a wonderful way.

October 2

YOU ARE MY EXPRESSION. Your immersion in Me overflows, spilling on those around you. As you rest in My goodness the peace you have will bring comfort to a troubled world. Know My impact through you matters greatly. Never be dismayed or discouraged; keep the awareness of who I am in and for you and darkness will flee, bringing light to others.

October 3

YOUR FAILURES DO NOT UNDERCUT YOUR VALUE TO ME. Quit allowing them to paint your experience. Focus on My love for you. You are Mine and I stand with you eternally. Rest in the acknowledgement of that and you will see transformation. Realize righteousness is yours by way of the Cross and then your mistakes will not determine your identity. Instead, the promise that I will complete the good work I have begun in you will manifest.

October 4

THE HORIZON IS ALWAYS AHEAD, AND THE SUN RISES DAILY. See the hope in that for your life. I am with you and failure cannot last as you lean into Me. Opportunities are constant for a good choice. You are just one step away from a beautiful beginning.

October 5

THE TREADMILL OF WORKS FOR APPROVAL MUST COME TO AN END. Know there is a freedom I paid for you to enter. Slavery ended at the Cross. Your emancipation is a reality. I will uncover the treasures within you as you rest in Me. Your design was redeemed when you rose with Me on resurrection day.

October 6

MY LOVE IS ETERNALLY STRONG TO UNDO THE EFFECTS OF A MEAN WORLD. You were in My sights before creation. I hold onto you with great care. See that whatever scarred you is no contest for Me. My intent to have you whole is real. The resurrection life I paid for is within you. It will transform and renew you as you become aware of its glorious fire to burn the cords that have had you bound.

October 7

THE MISTREATMENT OF YOU DOES NOT GO UNNOTICED BY ME. The value I place on you far exceeds what you experience in callous hands. I too have known uncaring hearts around Me. Trust Me to be there as your strength. We are joined together, and you are not alone. Rely on Me and know My peace within you is transformative and will change the situation in time.

October 8

I **AM FAITHFUL.** As you give Me preeminence in your life My light within you shines into your dark areas and brings growth and abundance. The smallness of your old independent life will give way to the largeness of the life we share. Our union was paid for at the Cross. The wealth of who I am became yours. Draw your identity from Me. I am your true source and have destined you to flourish.

October 9

Y OU ARE NOT ALONE. Know there was no distance that could keep Me away from the nearness I desired with you. My journey into creation, into the human experience, was for you. The Cross tore open the dark encasement that had you trapped. Within My resurrection and ascension, I carried you up to new creation reality where you are safely secured to My heart. Your feeling of alienation will dissolve at the realization of our union.

October 10

THE DOVE LANDS UPON YOU. You receive the light of the last Adam. Washed by Holy blood you are purified to claim your inheritance. Laying down old things that hinder, embrace new creation life never touched before by the darkness. Bare hearted, walk to My pulse lifting up the days to unfurl My message of love and truth.

October 11

YOUR ENTRANCE THROUGH THE CROSS SOLIDIFIES YOUR STANDING. You working to be acceptable to Me is unnecessary for I accept you always. Step into My approval of you and see shortcomings and sins fall away. Rejoice in My enjoyment of you. Your journey is to be an exploration of My love that flows continually, not a task to prove your own worth. My blood has already made you worthy.

October 12

YOUR DISAPPOINTMENT IN YOURSELF IS MISPLACED. The journey in Me overrides mistakes that were nailed to the Cross a long time ago. As the Israelites looked to the serpent on the pole, see Me crucified for you to find relief. The poison from snakes of failure cannot harm you. You are made new as you refuse to look away from Me. Keep your gaze constant and you will find victory.

October 13

TUNE OUT THE DRONING OF WORLDLY VOICES THAT CAUSE INSECURITY, ANXIETY, AND FEAR. Instead listen for My song over you. Its melody is designed to carry you to new places of victorious discovery. Hear that you were chosen long ago to be Mine and that treasures line the path before you. As you step out into the rhythm of My love, the good life I have prepared will come forth.

October 14

I AM THE WAY INTO REDEMPTION FROM ANY BAD THOUGHT OR ATTITUDE. My death on the Cross paved the way for you to be set free from debilitating patterns. Let go of offense and emerge into the liberating life of My design. Your likeness to Me is your destiny. I love. Focus on and receive that love and it will become the fabric of your life.

October 15

IF YOU COULD SEE THE UNION WE SHARE, YOU WOULD NOT BE AFRAID. The vastness of who I am is for you in every way. Take time to gaze at the Cross. I vanquished the forces against you. You were accepted in My heart with great joy. I have equipped you with My own resurrection life. Take courage and believe negative circumstance will part like the Red Sea. You will walk by walls of turbulent waves in complete victory.

October 16

TEAR DOWN THE THINGS THAT BLOCK YOUR VIEW OF ME. Take a bulldozer and get moving. Selfish desires of revenge, self-centered pity, or anything of the sort must go. Make way for glorious construction of My design.

October 17

YOU HAVE A SECURE PLACE IN My HEART. Nothing can dislodge you. Your wrong actions are not stronger than the Cross. Allow My redemption to set you free from sin. For you are no longer a slave; My body was broken to make you whole and liberated. Resurrection life is within you. See yourself as a new creation and sin will lose its hold.

October 18

IRE TOUCHED, I HAVE LIT YOU TO BURN WITH MY LIFE. The cold darkness of who you were before has been replaced by a heavenly blaze. Aglow in the Kingdom realize you are a messenger put in the world to bring forth My warmth and light.

October 19

IN MY HEART IS PLENTY OF SPACE FOR YOU TO CURL UP AND REST. When you are tired and weary, come. It is a place prepared for you at all times. The strain of trying circumstances will be eased when you enter in. I stand guard and watch over you with tender care. As you arise to go forth you will find you are replenished and made ready to face whatever lies ahead.

October 20

MY RESCUE OF YOU WAS PLANNED BEFORE TIME. With perseverance I came into the world to claim My own. The Cross undid sin's captivity of you. So, lift up your head and take heart. Sin has no real authority. I am your author, and you are pure before My eyes. Hold onto how I see you and sin will be diminished and the beauty of who I created you to be will come forth in your life.

October 21

YIELD TO MY LOVE; ALLOW IT TO BATHE THOSE PLACES IN YOURSELF THAT FEEL ALONE AND INADEQUATE. I am bigger than any insufficiency. Before time I chose you. You are an expression of My dream. Wake up to the fact that we are joined together in an invincible union. The territory before you is full of promise. Rise up and walk in My capability. In your weakness I am strong. You are more than able to take the land.

October 22

IN YOUR PAIN, KNOW I BORE IT WITH YOU ON THE CROSS. You are not alone at the mercy of cold circumstances. My embrace of you can be felt as you look My way. I am the source that will see you through. The sun will rise again in your heart and the light of the morning will be there, awakening you to the hope of a new day.

October 23

TAKE COURAGE FOR I FACED DOWN DEATH AND I LIVE WITHIN YOUR HEART. My guidance is there for you each day. Look into My word that will unloose lies that tie you to fear. You are not a victim. The victory of Calvary paved the way for resurrection life to flow within you. Power from on high is at your disposal.

October 24

THE CRUELTY OF THE PAST WILL LOSE ITS PLACE IN YOUR HEART AS YOU FOCUS ON THE CROSS, WHERE I ABSORBED SIN, PAIN, AND DEATH. My forgiveness there can become yours. Its freeing force will lift you up from the death of anger and resentment. Learn that resurrection life is transforming. What kept you locked in a tomb will be undone; you will come out into the light of a new day.

October 25

THERE ARE OTHERS AROUND YOU WHO NEED LOVE. Open your eyes and I will show you. Enlarge your heart with compassion, let go of the harsh judgments the world delights in. See how I see and reach out to the unwanted in your midst. Discover in Me all are wanted.

October 26

I WILL DEFEND YOU. I staked My life on you at the Cross. I found you worthy of the greatest sacrifice. Those that oppose My light in you will be subdued in time. The world is no match against Me. Look away from your weaknesses and hurts to Me alone. I equip you like no other. My vision for you is glorious. Surrender earthly cares for heavenly truths and your life will become victorious.

October 27

THE DEPTH OF WHO I AM CAN TRANSFORM YOU AS YOU SEEK ME WITH YOUR WHOLE HEART. Put aside all that would distract, stay laser focused on Me and you will find all you need to flourish. As you perceive My power it will instill you with the strength you need to overcome in all situations. Your life will not be small but large, full of life-giving properties to those around you.

October 28

KIND AND GOOD THOUGHTS BRING A HARVEST OF PEACE AND JOY. Learn to cultivate them daily. When negative, unkind, and critical thoughts arise weed them out quickly. If allowed to grow they will spread and overtake the garden. You are the gardener of your life and can bring forth great produce to benefit others or an empty haul that will help no one. It is your choice.

October 29

OUR HISTORY IS IN MY HEART AND I CAN TURN AROUND THE PAIN IF YOU TRUST ME. Forgiveness is the key. Release yourself from the prison of resentment and bitterness. Open the door. Come into the fresh air of hope and new opportunity. Good things are ahead as you allow My love to lead you.

October 30

DO NOT BE DISAPPOINTED IN YOURSELF; GO DEEPER INTO THE UNION WE SHARE. Know that I work all things together for your good. You are safe regardless of your failure. The future is one of promise as you look to Me. I am crafting in you something wonderful. Your design was in My heart before creation. My intent will come to pass. Walk with optimism. Place insecurity and regret behind you and see the beautiful possibility of your life unfold.

October 31

YOU NEED TO DRAW YOUR IDENTITY FROM ME, NOT FROM OTHER PEOPLE'S IMPRESSION OF YOU. Reckon yourself dead to all that you know is not of Me. Step out of those things and let them disintegrate behind you. Enter into the radiant future that is yours each day. I want to take you deeper into the exquisite radiance of who I am. Do not listen to any lies that come into your thoughts. Attack them with the true facts that you are Mine and I am pleased with you. The sword of the spirit is a mighty weapon to wield. As you listen to My advice and continue to put it into practice you will grow.

" Enter His gates with thanksgiving and His courts with praise; give thanks to Him and praise His name. For the Lord is good and His love endures forever; His faithfulness continues through all generations. "

Psalm 100:4-5 (NIV)

November

Thankfulness is a way of
life I carry within Me for
you. Cherish My careful
consideration for you and
let thankfulness arise within
your heart. As you do it
sends ripples of beauty
through heaven.

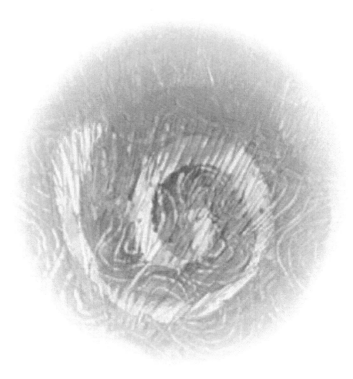

November 1

AS YOU GO ALONG DO NOT FEEL **NEGLECTED.** Your pilgrimage is very dear to Me. There is intense care and focus on you. Open your eyes to the revelation that royal blood was poured out on your behalf. You are of the utmost importance to Me for I planned you from the beginning. Your destiny is golden, no matter the opposition from the earthly realm. Your seat is in heavenly places so keep your vantage point above on the immense love of the One who died for you.

November 2

THE TIME YOU SPEND WITH ME WILL OPEN BEAUTIFUL VISTAS. You will see the beauty of creation, rolling hills, colorful squares of farmland, crystal lakes like blue eyes reflecting the sun. Yes, you will enter lands you would never get to explore on your own. Your heart, devoted to Me, is your compass.

November 3

I KNOW YOU. I see who you really are. My vision of you is eternal. The darkness that blocks your sight of your true identity will be lit up by My word that declares you My favored one. Lies that entangle you to worldly definition of failure have no reality. Your royalty in My Kingdom is secure. The destiny to rule and reign is your portion. Link yourself to this heavenly perspective and you will override the negatives that have no real lasting power.

November 4

THERE IS A FIERY TRUTH THAT A GOLDEN LIFE HAS BEEN PROVIDED FOR YOU. Penetrating love will purify you as you surrender your earthly rights to a heavenly order. No longer your own, you are joined to Me. All things that are good are possible in this union.

November 5

Y LOVE IS MORE POWERFUL THAN YOUR FEAR. Loosen your grip and let go into My strength that holds you. The world's voice is a stranger that knows you not. Quit listening and hear only Me. I am the one with the comfort and guidance you need.

November 6

THE RESURRECTION WAS FOR YOU. It lifted you up from a defeated life. You exist above circumstances no matter what it seems. Your security in Me is more real than the insecurity of the world. Rest in My goodness towards you and see it manifest in your life.

November 7

THE GIFT OF RIGHTEOUSNESS IS THE FLAMING TRUTH THAT IGNITES YOUR FREEDOM. The law has been fulfilled by Me and you are Mine. At the Cross the futile system of rules that enslaved you to failure was nailed there. You rose with Me into the liberty of a new life. Now trust Me within you to conform you into who I see you to be. Allow your behavior to flow from the acceptance and love I give you. As you do you will shine with the light of who I am in you.

November 8

~

REE OF LIFE LIVING IS YOUR DESTINY. Step out of the smaller realm where you are in charge of every move you make for good or ill. There is a more expansive place prepared for you as you learn to rest from your own labor. I finished the work for you to experience freedom.

November 9

I AM TRUE AND FAITHFUL. Release old hurts to Me and transformation will come. Your captivity to the past is not My desire. The Cross shows My identification with you in your pain. But resurrection reveals the life I paid for you to have. There are good things prepared as you embrace new patterns of forgiveness and hope. The horizon is bright and full of possibilities.

November 10

ONSTANT FIXATION ON YOURSELF CAN CREATE A STAGNANT EXISTENCE. Extend your sight to others who have needs as well. My life was laid down for those around you. As you begin to care, your life will develop to one of rich meaning.

November 11

THE LIFE I OFFER IS FULL OF ADVENTURE. The height and depth of Me is endless to explore. My death and resurrection opened new opportunities for you to experience a radically different way than the small dimensions of the world system. You have been translated into a beautiful mystery, a Kingdom that cannot be shaken. You are a member of a heavenly community. Your orders drip with the love of who I am. My ways overturned death. You too overturn death wherever you go. Life giving forces pulsate within you. Your task is a joyous one to infiltrate the world with love and laughter.

November 12

WHEN YOU FEEL LACK BELIEVE THE SUPPLY IS AT HAND, CLOSER THAN YOUR BREATH. You are not empty but have the fullness of who I am within you. Allow My peace to guide you and as you take steps fulfillment will come.

November 13

DO NOT LET DISCOURAGEMENT SET IN WHEN CIRCUMSTANCES PILE AGAINST YOU. Realize I am what is real in your life. I do not come and go. Focus on who I am in you and eventually the outside things will come into alignment. As you persevere My character is revealed in you. Take heart and have hope.

November 14

YOU ARE **M**Y PURSUIT. I took you into Myself on the Cross and extinguished what kept you from Me. Now you are entitled to all that I am and have for you. It is a never-ending journey into the majesty. In anticipation, let go of all that would weigh you down and run with speed into My arms of love.

November 15

*I*F YOU FEEL FRAGILE COME TO ME. I am the strength you need. You were sourced in Me as I alone cherished you in My heart before the ages. Breathe in the wind of My encouragement. Let it dislodge disappointment and regret. You are more than you know. We are inseparably joined. I am the architect of creation within, in which you have an integral and marvelous part.

November 16

WHEN YOU FEEL YOU ARE SLIPPING REALIZE I AM RESOLUTE WITHIN YOU TO KEEP YOU. Determine to look past your fears to the enormity of My love. It far outweighs the temporary senses that distort the truth. Reality is that you are solidly secured to Me.

November 17

LET THE CROSS BE YOUR FOCAL POINT WHEN YOU ARE IN A PAINFUL PLACE. I do not neglect your life. I identify like no other. I bore the depth of darkness to be with you now. You are not alone and never will be. You are greatly loved by Me. Death did not hold Me and cannot dictate the truth to you. My life, with resurrection power in you, is the truth.

November 18

WHEN YOU HAVE MADE A MISTAKE, I AM HERE. Come to Me and know I will make room for new growth and new beginnings. Place everything in My hands and see the power of resurrection, a truth that exists in all eternity at work in your circumstance. What was a loss, in My economy, will become a gain.

November 19

TAKE EXPECTATION OFF OF THOSE AROUND YOU. Seek your supply from Me alone. I am jealous for your devotion for it will empower your life to new levels. The wonder of who I am will enrich your existence. Give yourself to My love. Line up with My Cross and know resurrection life is yours. You were joined with Me there and what others do or do not do will lose the power to unsettle you.

November 20

LIFE IS YOURS AS A GIFT FROM ME. Live it knowing I am within you to secure you to victory. Never leave the awareness of My love for you. My love has amazing capacities to transform your daily existence into a beautiful adventure where you spread loveliness and life wherever you go.

November 21

THE CROSS WAS TO SHOW YOU THE DEPTH OF MY LOVE. Your redemption was My greatest desire. Realize I paid for your deliverance. Access the life that is yours and you never have to be constricted by law and performance again. You are free to radically thrive in a resurrected life. Seated above circumstances your life is one with Mine.

November 22

MY HEART FOR YOU IS DEEPER THAN THE DEEPEST OCEAN. Do not diminish the beauty I have crafted in you by bad thoughts of yourself. You are a diamond to Me that shines and reflects the light. Connect with how I see you and come into My delight of you.

November 23

DO NOT LIVE FROM THE TREE OF THE KNOWLEDGE OF GOOD AND EVIL MEASURING YOUR LIFE BY YOUR FAILURES OR SUCCESSES. Instead, keep your eye on My success, the Tree of Life within you. Eat the fruit from the tree that nourishes and supplies the beauty of who I am and who I declare you to be.

November 24

YOU ARE NOT THE ONLY ONE WHO HAS BEEN TORN. Learn to become a mender to those around you and you will find healing for yourself. My love is meant to flow. Receive it into your heart and let it go in all directions encountering everybody you meet. Your life will come into the wholeness that I designed for you.

November 25

SAVAGE WINDS WILL BLOW, AND THE RAIN WILL FALL BUT KNOW YOUR ROOTS GO DOWN INTO THE ETERNAL ROCK. Planted in a Holy Kingdom storms cannot overcome you. You will only get stronger. The light within you will bring forth a new day, one where the sun shines, a rainbow is seen, and great promise extends before you.

November 26

THE PAIN YOU ARE IN RIGHT NOW WILL BE IN THE PAST ONE DAY. Believe that you are not alone. The Cross showed Me where you are. There I defeated death on your behalf. Resurrection is set in motion for you to be lifted from the torment that seems insurmountable. Nothing on earth can separate you from Me. I am a faithful benefactor that establishes a hope filled future for you.

November 27

AKE THE TIME TO REALIZE MY LOVE FOR YOU EACH DAY. . It is ongoing and powerful to fortify you. Adversity will come but know your position in My heart is unshakable. Allow it to be a place of security. Your destiny will unfurl like a glorious banner, flapping in the wind; all will know you are Mine.

November 28

Y OU HAVE BEEN RECONCILED TO ME. There is nothing that places you on the outside. Focus on the warmth of My acceptance. Allow it to permeate your being. Mistakes and failure do not exclude you. Quit allowing them preeminence. Let My love reign with its cleansing and restorative power.

November 29

IN THE DARK CALL TO ME FOR YOU ARE OF MY KINGDOM. The glowing embers of orange and gold will keep you warm as I have sealed you with a fiery love. The cold arms of death in this life cannot grasp you because eternity burns brightly in your heart.

November 30

I WILL ARISE IN YOUR HEART AND UNLOCK THE PAIN WHEN YOU BEGIN TO SEE I AM HERE FOR YOU. I long to set you free but you must trust Me. I am not against you. I am your restorer and replenisher. It is a new day, and you are going to walk free.

" Then the angel said to them, 'Do not be afraid, for behold, I bring you good tidings of great joy which will be to all people. For there is born to you this day in the city of David a Savior, who is Christ the Lord. And this will be the sign to you: You will find a Babe wrapped in swaddling cloths, lying in a manger.' And suddenly there was with the angel a multitude of the heavenly host praising God and saying: 'Glory to God in the highest, and on earth peace, goodwill toward men!' "

Luke 2:10-14 (NKJV)

December

The snow is falling, the forest is still, moonlight is glistening on the face of the lake. A cabin is near with a warm fire dancing. Hot chocolate in a mug is waiting for you with Me to celebrate the season where I came to earth to be with you.

December 1

ENTRANCE IS OPEN TO MY THRONE ROOM. You are welcome there at any time. When life's circumstances press upon you step in and receive divine attention. My love acts as a cleanser washing away the world's residue replacing it with a heavenly shine.

December 2

IN ME YOU ARE BREATH TOUCHED, ENFOLDED IN LOVE, WASHED CLEAN AND NEW. Sparkling with life, My Spirit ignites levels of love that pour out in motion. The word of light is a two-edged sword breaking off the darkness in this world that clings closely. You are encapsulated in My blood, a bright light in you is ablaze to make darkness flee.

December 3

THE WORLD CAN BE HARSH; YOU CAN BE BYPASSED BUT IN ME YOU ARE HIGHLY VALUED. Draw your identity from My approval only. My love is the fuel you need to manage your life. Open your ears to hear My kindness. The awareness of the favor I have for you will manifest as you find your security in Me. Believe the plans I have for you are good.

December 4

IN THE AGONY OF WHERE YOU ARE, I AM THERE. The Cross is My identification with the pain you are experiencing. Be aware of the depth of My heart for you right now. You are not alone and never will be. Resurrection light is My promise. Know you are also with Me in the victory I had over death. The manifestation of that will materialize in your life.

December 5

THIS IS A NEW DAY. Surge into the place I have for you. Do not sit. Move forward with intent to spread My Kingdom. I am empowering you to feats that will bring light to those in darkness. Keep moving through barriers that have stopped you before. I will be with you as you break them down and gain new territory.

December 6

WHEN SOMEONE IS PUTTING YOU DOWN, COME TO ME. I have the supply you need. I will fortify you with truth and clarity. I am on your side. My love for you is intense and everlasting. The light of who you are in Me will prevail as your focus stays on My acceptance and approval.

December 7

Y UNDYING LOVE IS UPON YOU.
I fought and defeated death for you.
Remember that you are never alone but have been
called into the service of light. The darkness of the
world cannot overcome you for you are selected
to bear glorious fruit. Dwell in Me and allow My
nature to come forth as you lay your life down for
the victory of the Cross.

December 8

YOU ARE IN MY ROYAL BLOODLINE SO NEVER FEEL IMPOVERISHED. I invested My life into you for I saw you worthy. Lift your focus from your faults to the abundance of who I am. See us as one. Believe I am powerful to transform anything in you that does not line up with that truth.

December 9

YOUR NEXT BREATH IS FROM ME. Your next heartbeat is from Me. I sustain you. I love you and mean for you to be aware of that love. Seize the truth of My reality without which you would not exist. I chose you to exist with Me. Any blindness to our union must be healed by the light of who I am. My love knows no bounds. The boundaries in your heart are unnecessary. Look My way, open the gate, and allow My life to enrich you.

December 10

THE CROSS TESTIFIES OF THE LOVE THAT CALLED YOU WORTHY TO BE JOINED TO ME. Within My death all that separated you was taken away. Now you are truly alive, co-risen with Me. Your place in the Kingdom is far above. The world can no longer dictate to you who you are. My royal bloodline defines you.

December 11

YOUR LOVE IS VALUABLE. It can lighten the load of another and bring light into someone's day. Never take for granted the impact you can have as a conduit of My life. I have called you into a Kingdom that advances in the kindness you extend.

December 12

THANKFULNESS IS A DOOR TO MORE OF ME. A song of gratitude in your heart releases the music of heaven to beautify your life. Tremendous strides are made when you focus on the good. Rejoice for My enrichment of you is ongoing. Your praises will release the richness of who I am in you and will overflow to all you encounter.

December 13

YOU ARE MY DESIRE. The Cross points to My determination to have you. There is nothing that can separate you from Me. Relinquish thoughts that say you are neglected for I always have eyes for you. I see who you truly are and are designed to be. The world will crank out lies but you must have ears for only Me. My words sparkle and give life. Receive them as manna and let them nourish you. They will help you to flourish. I say you are fearfully and wonderfully made for My purposes. Rest knowing that they will be fulfilled in your life.

December 14

THE PATH THROUGH YOUR DAY WILL
LEAD TO GOOD THINGS AS YOU
CONSULT ME IN THE WAY TO GO. My insight
enlightens your experience. On your own, your
vision is dimmer. As you listen to My voice your
life expands and becomes fruitful.

December 15

SURRENDER YOUR WORRIES AND FEARS. Quit holding onto them as your friends. They are not and never will be. Instead focus on Me and the love I displayed on the Cross. The fierceness of My heart for you even moved the mountain of death. I am aware of your situation and as you lean into Me the heaviness of your experience will lighten. Peace is My gift in the midst of all circumstances.

December 16

LET NO SHADOW BLOCK MY TRUTH IN YOU. Your depth is greatly needed. See within your heart the sterling quality of silver, shining, that reflects My glory. Arise and come forth. That is who you truly are.

December 17

MY IDENTIFICATION WITH YOU IS REAL. I walked on earth to fully know you and to reveal My heart to you. You were the goal of the incarnation. The climax of the Cross destroyed our separation. Now we are joined eternally. The glory I have I gladly give. You shine with My light. Do not let dark thoughts corrupt the truth of that.

December 18

STAY WITH ME IN THE HARD TIMES. Focus on My love no matter the distance you feel, and I promise the warmth of heaven will soon thaw the circumstances that seem unbearable. Know My faithfulness is a certainty in life.

December 19

MY EMBRACE OF YOU IS REAL. I hold you in My heart tenderly. In the down times the veil of the world casts shadows upon this truth. You must reach through to the eternal fire of My love when the cold chill of darkness begins to close around you. I burn with desire for you to be freed from the constructs that blind you to the fact that I am here as your deliverer.

December 20

~

YOUR GUILT WENT WITH ME TO THE CROSS AND WAS DONE AWAY WITH THERE. Condemning thoughts are dead ends. Instead, focus on Me and who I say you are. Rise up into My approval of you and behavior that conflicts with that will fall away. The fact that you are a new creation supersedes anything of the old Adam. You are in My divine line which guaranties a fruitful life and a beautiful story.

December 21

GRATITUDE ENERGIZES GOOD THINGS TO COME. Focusing on the blessings in your life beautifully shapes your path. Grumblers and complainers, who emphasize the worst, make situations darker and get caught in webs of negativity. Resist the urge to go that route. Instead, weave light into your day with praise and thanksgiving.

December 22

EAR ME ALONE. Close off the voice of the tormenter. Strong words of encouragement and wisdom flow in a river from My throne room into your heart if you would only be still. Be perceptive and alert to golden instructions that continually come your way. I am alive and preside over the whole universe. I know what you need. Have faith that you are in My care. Rest in the love I have for you. Be comforted that you have My attention and that your life is never hidden from Me.

December 23

SLIPPING INTO JOY, DO NOT CATCH YOURSELF. Fall into My laughter. Warm folds of a soft blanket in My heart cradle you. Rest and live there. It is your home. I made you.

December 24

FILL YOURSELF WITH THOUGHTS OF WHO I AM AND WITH THE FERVENCY OF MY LOVE FOR YOU. Cut through the static of the world's philosophy with its impersonal platitudes, devoid of the message of the Cross. The Cross reverberates through time and gives validity to the worth of your existence. Your value was worth the expense of the rescue. The world's definition of you pales in comparison.

December 25

~

IN THE SNOW-COVERED FIELD ON A SILENT NIGHT, SEE THE STAR THAT LED TO THE WONDER OF A NEWBORN ONE NESTLED AGAINST THE WARMTH OF HIS MOTHER. You are Mine. Feel the warmth I enfold you in. The star now shines in your heart.

December 26

YOU WERE ENVISIONED IN MY HEART BEFORE THE FOUNDATION OF THE WORLD. Within Me be encouraged this day for you are empowered by unquenchable love. Nothing in the temporal realm can stop the force of it. Your life is called out and declared worthy. Walk accordingly, knowing that I am creating in you the golden character you are destined to become.

December 27

I AM RIGHT HERE IN THE MIDST OF YOUR PAIN. On the Cross I experienced great depths of torment so I could be with you like no other. Draw from Me. My love is tangible and can ease your situation. Become aware of My presence for the darkness cannot outlast My light.

December 28

BEFORE TIME, YOU WERE HIDDEN IN MY HEART. Your life was My desire. You are here at My request. Draw from the certainty of your importance to Me. Live courageously knowing I am for you. You are the prize I treasure.

December 29

B E KIND TO YOURSELF. Brutal thoughts that demean you are not coming from the throne room. I see you as lovely and worthwhile. Any self-concept less than that must go. You are created with great intent. Seize the truth of who I say you are and rise up and shine.

December 30

THE RULES YOU PUT YOURSELF UNDER HAVE NO POWER TO TRANSFORM YOU. It is My life in you that brings the change you desire. Rest in My unconditional love and favor. Those behaviors that make you feel condemned will meet their match in who I am in you. They lose their steam as you realize your true life is with Me in the union we share. The power that created the universe is within you and at your disposal. You are no longer helpless against the dictates of sin. The victory of the Cross is yours as well as resurrected and ascended life.

December 31

YOU ARE SO WORTH MY DEATH ON THE CROSS. My joy of you cannot be contained. Tap into the laughter of heaven that rejoices in your life. Smile with the knowing you are happily Mine forever.

Epilogue

In rest, the land spreads her blanket of green pastures. The gentle sheep graze. The sun is visited by laughing clouds. The swing from the tree of life beckons me to sit. In childlike motion I begin to move back and forth under a lush canopy of leaves in the strong arms of the tree. My soul hums with delight. Joy has returned to me. The Lion and the Lamb lay down together. The wind whispers love songs older than time that I have always been cherished. It is all good. You have rescued me from fearful hectic days and dull sleepless nights. I now realize I have always safely been in Your heart, under Your constant care.

Made in the USA
Coppell, TX
07 June 2022